I LOVE CRAB CAKES!

# I LOVE
# CRAB CAKES

## 50 Recipes for an American Classic

### TOM DOUGLAS

*with Shelley Lance*

PHOTOGRAPHS BY ROBIN LAYTON

WILLIAM MORROW
*An Imprint of HarperCollinsPublishers*

HarperCollins books may be purchased for educational, business, or sales promotional use. For information please write: Special Markets Department, HarperCollins Publishers, 10 East 53rd Street, New York, NY 10022.

**FIRST EDITION**

DESIGNED BY *Lorie Pagnozzi*

Printed on acid-free paper

Library of Congress Cataloging-in-Publication Data

Douglas, Tom, 1958–
I love crab cakes! : 50 recipes for an American classic / Tom Douglas.
p. cm.
ISBN-13: 978-0-06-088196-2
ISBN-10: 0-06-088196-8
1. Cookery (Crabs) I. Title.

TX754.C83D68  2006
641.6'95—dc22                                        2005056138

06 07 08 09 10  ◆/TP 10 9 8 7 6 5 4 3 2 1

*To my mom, Mary Douglas, who, when asked
where she goes for her favorite crab cakes, responded,
"Right in my kitchen, of course."*

★

# CONTENTS

# ACKNOWLEDGMENTS

I often say I'm lucky to be surrounded by many people I consider tops in the business. My whole team of 350 people who make up Tom Douglas Restaurants are an inspiration. Their contribution of family recipes and crab cake thoughts and ideas give this book breadth. Thanks to Eric Tanaka, Chris Fitzgibbon, and Julie Hartley, who were invaluable in the nuts and bolts testing of each and every recipe, over and over again.

A personal thanks to Shelley Lance, my longtime associate, recipe developer, and cowriter, I owe you a Negroni.

Acknowledgments all around to the dedicated team at HarperCollins: Leah Carlson-Stanisic, Lorie Pagnozzi, Lucy Baker, Karen Lumley, Roberto de Vicq de Cumptich, and Carrie Bachman. Kudos to my editor, Harriet Bell, for finally realizing that life begins not on Manhattan island but on Orcas Island.

To my friend and agent, Judith Riven, and my personal "nanny," Amy Pennington: Thanks for keeping all directions that my life takes moving forward.

Many thanks to our awesome photographer, Robin Layton, who has a great eye, and to the stylin' Christy Nordstrom on props. To my chef buddies across the country who participated with recipes, this book would not be nearly as fun without you.

Thanks also to my wife, Jackie Cross, who despite being allergic to crab, jumped right in and helped with every aspect of this book. And finally, to my daughter, Loretta, my favorite little crab cake eater.

# EVERYBODY LOVES CRAB CAKES

Where do you get the best crab cakes? Ask that question to a hundred people and you're likely to get a hundred different answers. Some New Yorkers swear by Pearl Oyster Bar in the West Village, while Marylanders would argue till the crabs come home about G&M, Timbuktu, or the Robert Morris Inn. Washington, D.C., Roanoke, Philly, and certainly every town on the Eastern Shore would be happy to join in the fray.

There are websites devoted to the art of the crab cake. Sweet creamy textures married to lumpfin, backfin, or body meat. Restaurants can be made or broken on their crab cake reviews. The rewards for the positive are lines out the door. Beware the poor fellow who gets dinged for using "too much filler," a common reference to too many crumbs in your cake, for he shall hang his head in shame. When I asked my mom, who still lives in Newark, Delaware (thirty minutes north of Chesapeake Bay), where she goes for her favorite crab cake, her response was swift and confident, "My kitchen!"

Every crab cake is a bit unique depending on area or creed. Are you a bread man or saltine fan, or no crumbs at all? Does deep-frying float your boat or a delicate panfry in whole sweet butter? Do you broil your crab cake so it doesn't fall apart? Do you like your crab cakes plattered with crispy fries and sweet-and-sour slaw? Or slapped on a plump bun with chunky dill pickle tartar sauce? Maybe you are an Old Bay traditionalist from Baltimore. Until I was nineteen years old I never ate a crab that had not been steamed with Old Bay. Since then I've come to crave other flavorings, such as herbes de Provence or Chinese black bean sauce.

When I moved to Seattle in 1977 from crab cake country, the mid-Atlantic home of the Chesapeake and Delaware Bays, it never occurred to me that in the Emerald City I wouldn't be able to find a crab cake. After all, Seattle is right on Puget Sound, the land of Dungeness crab, a sweet, briny, and meaty 3- to 4-pound beautiful monster of the Pacific Ocean. This is a city where you can walk out on the tide flats and literally grab a Dungie, and I couldn't find one damn crab cake! This was unfathomable to me, having gorged on crab cakes from Atlantic City to Virginia Beach. Crab shacks and crab cakes reign supreme from the most run-down boardwalks to the mightiest boardrooms.

Well, I fixed that! And what's more—I became a little famous for it. Stacks of gleaming crabs, cooked at sea and iced at every market or better yet, snappy Dungeness clinging to each other in saltwater live tanks, were all the inspiration I needed. With a menu full of exotic dishes like kasuzuke black cod with seaweed salad, and red chili pasta with salsa and spot prawns, it turned out my fresh Dungeness crab cakes, inspired by my stint at the Hotel du Pont in Wilmington, Delaware, seven years earlier, were hands down the big hit.

Twenty years later, crab cakes have become a national phenomenon. When I sent out a request to my chef buddies around the country for either a regional favorite or their personal favorite crab cake recipe, no one responded with a "Sorry, I don't make crab cakes." In fact, everyone from Jacques Pépin in Connecticut and Emeril Lagasse in New Orleans to Nancy Silverton in L.A. and Mark Bittman in N.Y.C. had a favorite recipe or style.

I am enamored with the variety and originality of our assembled crab cake recipes. Perfect combinations like Chris Schlesinger's Tidewater Cakes, spiked with southern Smithfield ham bits, taste like a boardinghouse staple. The tempura-seaweed crab cakes, deep-fried into sea forms, can easily be confused with creatures you'd see in the tanks at the Seattle Aquarium.

Have fun with this book. Break out now and then! You traditionalists will be thrilled with our Chesapeake Bay Classic, but don't be afraid to try the avant-garde Crab and Scallop Cakes Steamed in Banana Leaves or Tomato Aspic Crab Cakes, culled from memories of Grandma Fogarty's kitchen. Yes, it's old-fashioned, but also delicious.

Embrace this book for what it is—a look at a true American classic—the crab cake.

★

# HOW TO MAKE PERFECT CRAB CAKES: TECHNIQUES AND INGREDIENTS

## Which Crab to Use

*I Love Crab Cakes!* features crabs from all over North America. For all of the recipes, blue crab, Phillips brand pasteurized crab, and Dungeness crab are interchangeable. Jonah crab or Peekytoe also work well. King crab, while you can chop and use it, will give a different texture.

## Crabmeat

I like the body, leg, and claw meat of the Dungeness crab equally. Jumbo lump and backfin of the blue crab are the most sought after and make the best-textured crab cakes. I have found that the Phillips brand pasteurized crabmeat from Southeast Asia is an okay substitute, but fresh is always best.

## Draining and Squeezing Crabmeat

Drain the crabmeat in a sieve. Dungeness and King tend to be quite wet. Gently squeeze the crabmeat with your hands to remove excess liquid, and at the same time feel for any bits of cartilage or shell and remove them. There's a fine balance between wet crab and dry, stringy crab, and your

challenge is to remove moisture without drying out the crab too much.

## Mixing and Handling

Mix gently. Crabmeat is graded and priced on the size of the lumps, with lump meat often being double the price of body meat. Fold the crabmeat and the dressing together with a rubber spatula as if you're folding whipped cream into a mousse.

## Chilling Crab Cakes

Once shaped, most crab cakes will be easier to handle if you chill them awhile. You can leave them right in the pan of crumbs for at least 30 minutes or for several hours or even overnight. The crab cakes will continue to soak up more crumbs if you leave them sitting in a pan of crumbs for a long time, so only do this if you like a heavier crumb. Alternatively, you can refrigerate the crab mixture first, then scoop and crumb the cakes right before you plan to cook them.

## Forming Crab Cakes

A 2-ounce ice cream scoop is perfect for shaping a classic 2½- to 3-ounce cake. Buy a scoop with a release lever. Lightly pack the scoop with the heel of your hand and release the cake directly into the pan of bread crumbs. Press the crumbs around the cake while you're shaping it into a disk.

## Dredging Crab Cakes

You can turn the cakes on both sides in the crumbs, or if the cakes are soft or fragile, it may be easiest to set them in the pan and sprinkle crumbs or flour over the top. Each recipe includes an excess quantity of bread crumbs or flour for easy dredging. You can refrigerate the crab cakes right in the pan of bread crumbs, but if a crab cake recipe calls for dredging just in flour, don't dredge until you're ready to cook. Otherwise, a flour-dredged crab cake will absorb all the flour while it's in the refrigerator.

## Cooking Crab Cakes

The easiest way to tell if a crab cake is cooked is with an instant-read thermometer. Insert the thermometer into the center of the cake and if the temperature is 155°F, the crab cake is fully cooked.

Turn the crab cakes only once while cooking. Flip-flopping them is likely to break them apart and they won't get a nice crust.

For sautéing, a good, seasoned cast-iron pan, or a shiny stainless steel sauté pan like an All-Clad or KitchenAid, or a pan with a nonstick surface all work well.

For deep-frying, I prefer to use my wok and a spider (a Chinese mesh strainer) for scooping out the cakes.

## Salt

Some Dungeness and King crabs are very salty. Taste and adjust the salt in the recipe accordingly, especially if you're using Dungeness in a recipe that calls for blue or other crab.

## Freezing

Formed and uncooked crab cakes with a mayonnaise binder tend to freeze well since the oil in the mayonnaise protects the crabmeat. To freeze crab cakes, first completely form and crumb them. Then spread them in a single layer on a baking sheet and freeze. When they're solid, you can gather them into a scalable plastic freezer bag, with wax paper or parchment paper in between the cakes. Thaw in the refrigerator before cooking. I have had good luck freezing the Etta's Classic Dungeness Crab Cakes, for example.

## Banana Leaves

Banana leaves can be found frozen in sealed plastic bags in specialty Asian grocery stores. Thaw before using.

## Bread Crumbs, Fresh and Dried

I make fresh bread crumbs from supermarket white sandwich bread. Tear the bread into pieces (no need to remove the crusts since they're so tender) and process to fine crumbs in a food processor. Two slices of white sandwich bread make about 2 cups crumbs.

While some people prefer to use cracker crumbs in their crab cakes, I use my own homemade dried bread crumbs made from a crusty loaf of rustic white bread. A half loaf of European-style white bread (around 12 ounces or about 8 slices) yields 2½ cups bread crumbs. If you must use purchased bread crumbs, they should be "plain" crumbs only, not flavored.

Preheat the oven to 325°F. Cut the crusts off the bread and discard, then slice the bread ½ inch thick. Place the slices in a single layer on an ungreased baking sheet. Put the baking sheet in the oven and bake until the bread feels dried out in the center, about 40 minutes. Turn the bread over from time to time so it dries out evenly. Remove the bread from the oven and allow to cool. Tear the bread into pieces and place in a food processor. Pulse until the crumbs are very fine. Sieve the crumbs to remove any large pieces.

Dried bread crumbs will keep a week or more at room temperature in a tightly sealed container, or seal them in plastic bags and freeze them for a month or more.

## Chinese Chili Paste

There are many bottled Asian chili pastes on the market. We like the flavor of Lan Chi brand, which is made of chile peppers and oil with a nice kick of garlic. My very favorite brand has Chinese black beans in it, but no English brand name on the label.

## Chipotle Peppers

Chipotle peppers are smoked jalapeños. You can find canned chipotle peppers in adobo in Latino markets and many supermarkets. To make a puree, pour the contents of the can in a food processor and puree until smooth, then store in a jar in the refrigerator for a quick hit of flavor and heat. Or you can take a few chiles from the can and finely mince them, then mash them with a knife.

## Eggs and Egg Safety

Use very fresh Grade A or Grade AA eggs (check the expiration date on the label before buying) and always keep the eggs refrigerated. It's important to be aware of the potential dangers of salmonella and other harmful bacteria that may occur in eggs and take precautions. Don't keep eggs at room temperature for more than an hour, and always wash your hands, work surface, and equipment before and after using raw eggs. Use products that have been made with raw eggs within one day.

### Fish Sauce

Fish sauce is called nam pla in Thailand and nuoc mam in Vietnam. Made from salted fermented fish, these sauces add a pleasant, pungent, and salty undertone to many Asian dishes.

### Masa Harina

Masa harina is a flour made from dried and ground masa, which is the corn dough used for making tortillas. Often sold in paper bags, masa harina is available in Latino markets and many large supermarkets.

### Mayonnaise

When using purchased mayonnaise, I prefer Hellmann's or Best Foods.

### Mirin

This is a sweetened sake intended for cooking.

### Nori

These sheets of dried seaweed are used to wrap sushi and as a flavoring or garnish in Japanese cooking.

### Ogo and Seaweed Salad

Ogo is a crisp, crunchy seaweed, usually greenish in color, that's popular in Hawaiian cooking. Buy it fresh, when available. Seaweed salad (also called ocean salad) is a prepared salad composed of various types of seaweed, dressed with sesame oil and rice vinegar.

Both are sold in Japanese fish markets and specialty stores.

### Oil

For frying, I like canola, peanut, or grapeseed oils for their clean, neutral flavors and high smoke points.

### Old Bay Seasoning

The classic Chesapeake Bay seasoning blend for steaming blue crabs contains celery seeds, bay leaves, mustard, red pepper, and ginger, among other flavors. The name "Old Bay" is now owned by McCormick brand.

### Panko

Japanese bread crumbs are coarser than ordinary bread crumbs and stay nice and crisp when fried, making them perfect for dredging crab cakes. You can find panko in Japanese and other Asian markets, Japanese fish markets, and many large supermarkets (check the seafood department).

### Sambal

Sambal badjak and sambal olek are hot chili paste condiments used in Indonesian cooking. Sambal can be found in well-stocked supermarkets and Asian specialty stores.

### Shao Mai Wrappers

These round, very thin, wheat-flour wrappers are used to make dumplings that wrap around a filling, leaving the top exposed. They should be about 3 inches in diameter and very thin. In Seattle, we use the Rose brand shao mai wrapper.

### Spices, Toasted and Ground

I generally buy whole spices and grind them myself for better flavor. To heighten the flavor of certain spices, like cumin and coriander seeds, I toast them briefly before grinding them.

To toast spices, place them in a small, heavy skillet over medium heat for a few minutes, shaking or stirring constantly, just until they are very lightly browned and aromatic. Spices burn easily, so watch them carefully.

I use a separate electric coffee grinder for grinding spices. I keep one for my coffee and one just for spices. You can also use a mortar and pestle, which is fun to use, though it takes more muscle.

### Sriracha

Named for a seaside town in southern Thailand, sriracha is a mixture of chile, tomato, salt, garlic, sugar, and vinegar. It has a color and consistency similar to ketchup.

## Star Anise

This star-shaped seedpod with a sweet flavor and aroma is one of my favorite spices. Crush the pods with a rolling pin or grind them in a spice grinder or a clean electric coffee bean grinder.

## Sweet Chile Sauce

This is a thin, orange-red sauce made from pounded chiles, sugar, salt, oil, and vinegar. There are many brands from several Asian countries, but we like Mae Ploy brand sweet chile sauce from Thailand.

## Thai Curry Paste

Thai curry pastes are sold in small cans, jars, and plastic tubs. We like the Mae Ploy brand. The curry pastes are classified by color: red, green, and yellow. These are complex mixtures containing chile peppers, lemongrass, shallots, garlic, galangal, coriander roots, shrimp paste, and other ingredients. Red curry paste has good flavor and medium heat.

## Tobiko

Tobiko is flying-fish roe. The tiny golden eggs of the flying fish add a delicious salty crunch to many sushi preparations.

## Tomatoes, Peeled, Seeded, and Diced

The easiest way to peel tomatoes is to core them, cut an X in the bottom, then plunge them in boiling water for a few seconds. Remove them from the boiling water with a slotted spoon and immediately plunge them into a bowl of ice water. Remove the tomatoes from the ice water, and the peels will slide off easily with your fingers or a paring knife.

When dicing tomatoes, always seed them first so the watery juices don't dilute the finished dish. To seed before dicing, core the tomato and slice it in half across the diameter, then squeeze out all the seeds, using your fingers or a small spoon to dig out and discard all the seeds and juices. Cut the tomato flesh into dice.

# AMERICAN

# CRAB

# CAKES

# ETTA'S CLASSIC DUNGENESS CRAB CAKES

*Makes 8 large crab cakes*

I've been serving these crab cakes at my restaurants, first at Dahlia Lounge and then at Etta's, since we opened more than seventeen years ago. They've consistently been a top seller, and I can't imagine that I'll ever take them off the menu.

1 large egg yolk

2 teaspoons fresh lemon juice

2 teaspoons Worcestershire sauce

1½ teaspoons Tabasco

2 tablespoons plus 1 teaspoon Dijon mustard

½ teaspoon paprika

½ teaspoon chopped fresh or dried thyme

½ teaspoon celery seeds

¼ teaspoon freshly ground black pepper

5 tablespoons olive oil

5 cups fresh bread crumbs (page 7)

¾ cup chopped parsley

¼ cup chopped onion

¼ cup chopped green bell pepper

¼ cup chopped red bell pepper

1 pound Dungeness crabmeat, drained, picked clean of shell, and lightly squeezed if wet (see page 5)

About 5 tablespoons unsalted butter

Green Cocktail Sauce (page 127)

4 lemon wedges

In a food processor or a blender, combine the egg yolk, lemon juice, Worcestershire, Tabasco, mustard, paprika, thyme, celery seeds, and black pepper. Pulse to combine. With the motor running, slowly add the oil through the feed tube until the mixture emulsifies and forms a mayonnaise. Set aside.

Put the bread crumbs in a shallow container and mix in ½ cup of the chopped parsley (reserve the remaining ¼ cup chopped parsley for the crab cake mixture). Set aside.

In a large bowl, combine the onion and bell peppers with the remaining ¼ cup parsley.

Add the reserved mayonnaise and the crabmeat and mix lightly to combine. Using a rubber spatula, fold in 1 cup of the bread crumb–parsley mixture. Do not overwork the mixture or the crab cakes may get gummy. Gently form 8 patties and dredge the patties lightly in the remaining bread crumb–parsley mixture. If you have time, cover the crab cakes with plastic wrap and chill for an hour or longer.

Place 2 large nonstick skillets over medium heat and add about 2½ tablespoons butter to each pan. As soon as the butter is melted, add 4 cakes to each pan. Gently fry the crab cakes until they are hot through and golden brown on both sides, turning once with a spatula, about 4 minutes per side. The internal temperature of a crab cake should be 155°F on an instant-read thermometer. Transfer the crab cakes to 4 plates and serve each plate with a ramekin of Green Cocktail Sauce and a lemon wedge.

# CHESAPEAKE BAY CLASSIC CRAB CAKES

*Makes 8 large crab cakes*

The traditional crabmeat to use in these Chesapeake Bay cakes is East Coast blue crab. If you can't get fresh crab, try the pasteurized crab usually sold in the refrigerated case of your supermarket or fish store, such as Phillips brand, which is not to be confused with shelf-stable canned crab.

If you live on the West Coast, this recipe works just fine with Dungeness, but you will probably need to squeeze out the excess liquid. If your Dungie tastes salty, you may want to omit the salt in the recipe because there's already salt in the Old Bay Seasoning.

Traditionally, these cakes are served with tartar sauce, but I prefer the tangy zip of green or red cocktail sauce to offset their creaminess.

**NOTE:** *If you love Maryland crab cakes that are broiled, but not breaded, this recipe works great. Increase the egg to 2 yolks, make the crab cake mixture, and shape into 8 cakes, omitting the step of dredging in bread crumbs. Refrigerate for 1 to 4 hours or overnight. Arrange the cakes in a pan and broil until they're hot through and lightly golden brown, 5 to 6 minutes, rotating the pan as needed to brown the cakes evenly. (The internal temperature of a crab cake should be 155°F on an instant-read thermometer.)*

1 large egg yolk

1 tablespoon Old Bay Seasoning (see page 10)

1 tablespoon Dijon mustard

1/2 teaspoon grated lemon zest

1 1/2 teaspoons fresh lemon juice

1 1/2 teaspoons cider vinegar

1/2 cup peanut or canola oil

1/4 teaspoon kosher salt

1/4 teaspoon freshly ground black pepper

1 tablespoon minced scallions, both white and green parts

1 pound lump blue crabmeat, drained and picked clean of shell

| 4 cups fresh bread crumbs (see page 7) | About 4 tablespoons unsalted butter | 4 lemon wedges |
|---|---|---|
| ¼ cup chopped parsley | Red Cocktail Sauce (page 126), Green Cocktail Sauce (page 127), or Really Good Tartar Sauce (page 128) | |

Put the egg yolk, Old Bay, mustard, lemon zest and juice, and vinegar in the bowl of a food processor or a blender and process until smooth. Gradually pour in the oil with the machine running until the mixture emulsifies and forms a mayonnaise. Season with the salt and pepper. (Note: This quantity of mayonnaise will not emulsify in the bowl of the largest food processor. Use a medium food processor, a mini processor, or a blender.)

Transfer the mayonnaise to a bowl and, using a rubber spatula, fold in the scallions and the crabmeat until well combined. Combine the bread crumbs and the parsley in a shallow container. Form the crab mixture into 8 patties about 3 inches wide and ¾ inch thick and drop them into the bread crumb–parsley mixture. Dredge the crab cakes on both sides. If you have time, leave the crab cakes in the container of bread crumbs, cover with plastic wrap, and chill for an hour or more.

When you are ready to fry the crab cakes, put 2 large nonstick skillets over medium heat. Add about 2 tablespoons butter to each pan. When the butter is melted, add 4 crab cakes to each pan, patting off excess crumbs first. Slowly fry the crab cakes until they are golden brown on both sides and hot through, turning once with a spatula, about 4 minutes per side. If the crab cakes are browning too quickly, reduce the heat. The internal temperature of a cooked crab cake should be 155°F on an instant-read thermometer.

Transfer the crab cakes to plates, 2 per person, and serve with your choice of sauce and lemon wedges.

# ETTA'S NEW DUNGENESS CRAB CAKES

*Makes 8 large crab cakes*

This is a lighter and creamier version of our Etta's Classic since all of the bread crumbs are on the outside of the cakes.

These cakes are soft and need at least an hour's chilling time before panfrying.

1 large egg yolk

1 tablespoon cider vinegar

1 tablespoon Dijon mustard

1 tablespoon finely chopped red bell pepper

1 tablespoon finely chopped onion

3 tablespoons plus 2 teaspoons chopped parsley

1 teaspoon Tabasco

½ teaspoon paprika

½ teaspoon chopped fresh thyme

¼ teaspoon kosher salt

¼ teaspoon freshly ground black pepper

¼ cup olive oil

¼ cup sour cream

1 pound fresh Dungeness crabmeat, drained, picked clean of shell, and lightly squeezed if wet (see page 5)

4 cups fresh bread crumbs (see page 7)

About 4 tablespoons unsalted butter

Green Cocktail Sauce (page 127)

4 lemon wedges

In a food processor, combine the egg yolk, vinegar, mustard, bell pepper, onion, the 2 teaspoons parsley, Tabasco, paprika, thyme, salt, and pepper. Pulse to finely mince the vegetables and combine all the ingredients. With the motor running, slowly add the oil through the feed tube until the mixture emulsifies and forms a thin mayonnaise. (Note: This amount of mayonnaise will not emulsify in the largest food processor. Use a medium processor, a mini processor, or mince the vegetables very fine and use a blender.)

Transfer the mayonnaise to a large bowl and stir in the sour cream, then use a rubber spatula to fold in the crabmeat. Gently form 8 patties, about 3 inches wide by ¾ inch thick. Put the bread crumbs in a shallow container and mix in the 3 tablespoons parsley. Lightly dredge the patties on both sides in the bread crumbs. Cover the crab cakes with plastic wrap and chill for at least 1 hour or longer.

Put 2 large nonstick skillets over medium heat and add about 2 tablespoons butter to each pan. When the butter is melted, add 4 crab cakes to each pan. Gently fry the crab cakes until they are golden brown on both sides and hot through, turning once with a spatula, about 4 minutes per side. The internal temperature of a crab cake should be 155°F on an instant-read thermometer.

Transfer the crab cakes to plates, serving 2 to each person, accompanied by ramekins of Green Cocktail Sauce and lemon wedges.

★

# STEVEN'S PERFECT DUNGENESS CRAB CAKES

*Makes 8 large crab cakes*

Steven Steinbock, my friend and coworker for well more than twenty years and one of the best cooks I know, makes a perfectly balanced crab cake with a beautiful hazelnut brown crust.

A few tips from Steven: To get the best crust, turn the crab cakes once while they're in the oven, but otherwise don't disturb them. Also, for the best flavor, squeeze a lemon wedge over the crab cakes right away while they're still hot.

| | | |
|---|---|---|
| 1 pound Dungeness crabmeat, drained, picked clean of shell, and lightly squeezed if wet (see page 5) | 2 tablespoons plus 2 teaspoons minced fresh dill | ½ cup panko (see page 10), plus 2 cups more for dredging |
| ½ cup plus 2 tablespoons mayonnaise, preferably Hellmann's or Best Foods | 2 tablespoons plus 2 teaspoons thinly sliced chives | About 5 tablespoons unsalted butter |
| 2 tablespoons plus 2 teaspoons grated lemon zest | ½ teaspoon kosher salt | Tomato-Avocado Salsa (page 135) |
| | ¼ teaspoon freshly ground black pepper | 4 lemon wedges |
| | | 4 dill sprigs |

To make the crab cakes, put the crabmeat, mayonnaise, lemon zest, dill, chives, salt, and pepper in a large bowl. Mix everything together gently with a rubber spatula. Add the ½ cup panko and mix again. Pour the remaining 2 cups panko into a shallow container.

Form the crab mixture into 8 patties. Pat them gently into shape without pressing them too much. Drop the patties into the panko and turn them to coat both sides, patting to shake off the excess. If you have time, cover with plastic wrap and chill the crab cakes in the refrigerator for 1 hour or more before frying.

When you are ready to fry the crab cakes, preheat the oven to 450°F. Put 2 large nonstick ovenproof skillets over medium-high heat and add about 2½ tablespoons butter to each pan. As soon as the butter is melted, add 4 crab cakes to each pan. Leave the pans on the burners for a minute or slightly less (the butter should not start to brown), then place the pans in the oven. Cook the crab cakes until they are heated through and golden brown on both sides, about 12 minutes, carefully turning them with a spatula about halfway through the cooking time. Remove the pans from the oven and transfer the crab cakes to plates, serving 2 crab cakes to each person. Garnish each plate with a big spoonful of Tomato-Avocado Salsa, a lemon wedge, and a dill sprig.

★

# EMERIL'S CRAB CAKES

*Makes 8 large crab cakes*

These flavorful crab cakes are a New Orleans classic. They're bound with béchamel sauce, which gives them a creamy texture, and of course they're packed with Louisiana flavors, like the "holy trinity" of onion, celery, and bell pepper inside the cakes and Creole spices in the dredging mixture. Serve them with Emeril's fantastic corn tartar sauce that you can make as spicy as you like.

7 tablespoons unsalted butter

2 tablespoons all-purpose flour

½ cup finely chopped green onions, green parts only

¼ cup finely chopped celery

¼ cup finely chopped red bell pepper

1 teaspoon kosher salt

¼ teaspoon cayenne

¼ teaspoon freshly ground black pepper

1 cup milk

2 tablespoons chopped parsley, plus 1 tablespoon more for garnish

1 large egg, beaten

1 pound lump blue crabmeat, drained and picked clean of shell

20 saltine crackers, finely crushed in a blender or food processor

1 cup dried bread crumbs (see page 7)

1 tablespoon Emeril's Creole Seasoning (see recipe below), or other Creole or Cajun seasoning

¼ cup peanut or canola oil

Spicy Corn Tartar Sauce (page 129)

1 cup mesclun greens

Melt 3 tablespoons of the butter in a large skillet over medium heat. Add the flour and cook, stirring, to make a light roux, about 2 minutes. Add the green onions, celery, bell pepper, salt, cayenne, and black pepper and cook, stirring, until the vegetables are soft, about 3 minutes. Slowly add the milk, stirring constantly, and bring to a boil. Reduce the heat and simmer, stirring, until the béchamel mixture thickens, about 4 minutes. Remove from the heat and stir in the 2 tablespoons parsley. Let cool a few minutes.

In a large bowl, combine the egg with the crabmeat and cracker crumbs, mixing gently so as to not break up the lumps. Fold in the béchamel mixture and let cool. Divide the mixture into 8 equal portions and shape into patties. If you have time, cover the patties with plastic wrap and refrigerate 30 minutes or more.

When you are ready to fry the crab cakes, combine the bread crumbs and Creole seasoning in a shallow container. One at a time, dredge the patties in the crumbs, turning to coat evenly, and place them on a large plate.

Put 2 large nonstick skillets over medium-high heat and add the remaining 2 tablespoons butter and 2 tablespoons oil to each pan. When the butter and oil mixture is hot, add 4 patties to each pan. Fry the cakes until golden brown and heated through, turning once with a spatula to brown both sides, 3 to 4 minutes per side, turning the heat down if the crab cakes are browning too fast. The internal temperature of a crab cake should be 155°F on an instant-read thermometer. Remove the crab cakes from the skillets and drain on paper towels.

Transfer the crab cakes to plates and serve, 2 per person, accompanied by the Spicy Corn Tartar Sauce. Garnish each plate with some of the mesclun greens and sprinkle with the reserved parsley. Serve immediately.

## EMERIL'S CREOLE SEASONING

*Makes about ⅔ cup*

| | | |
|---|---|---|
| 2 tablespoons plus 1½ teaspoons paprika | 1 tablespoon freshly ground black pepper | 1 tablespoon dried oregano |
| 2 tablespoons kosher salt | 1 tablespoon onion powder | 1 tablespoon dried thyme |
| 2 tablespoons garlic powder | 1 tablespoon cayenne | |

In a small bowl, combine all the ingredients thoroughly. Store in an airtight container at room temperature for up to 3 months.

*Makes 8 large crab cakes*

Whenever I'm at Costco, no matter whether I'm shopping for a miter saw or an office desk, somehow I always end up with a can of pasteurized Phillips brand crabmeat in my basket—must be something in my East Coast roots. In fact, every ingredient in this recipe is available at Costco, so it's a simple quick hit for supper when you get home. Best of all, kids love it because of the creamy, gooey, cheesy center.

The crab cakes can be cooked right away, but if you have time, chilling them for 30 minutes or more before frying will make them easier to handle.

If you serve these crab cakes over tortilla chips with salsa, it's just like eating crab nachos!

1 large egg

¼ cup sour cream

2 teaspoons chili powder

¼ teaspoon kosher salt

1½ cups grated Cheddar cheese

1 pound blue crabmeat, drained and picked clean of shell

3 cups fresh bread crumbs (see page 7)

¼ cup peanut or canola oil

Tomato-Avocado Salsa (page 135) or Roasted Tomatillo Salsa (page 136)

Using a whisk, beat the egg in a large bowl with the sour cream, chili powder, and salt. Add the cheese and the crabmeat and fold everything together, using a rubber spatula. Divide into 8 mounds and firmly form into patties, about 3 inches by ¾ inch. Put the bread crumbs in a shallow container and dredge the patties on both sides, patting off excess crumbs.

Put 2 large nonstick skillets over medium heat and add 2 tablespoons oil to each skillet. When the pans are hot, add 4 patties to each pan. Fry until golden brown and hot through, turning once with a spatula, about 4 minutes per side. The internal temperature of a crab cake should read 155°F on an instant-read thermometer.

Transfer the crab cakes to plates, 2 cakes per person, and serve with one or both salsas.

# AUNT MARION'S CRAB CAKES

*Makes 10 large crab cakes*

This cherished family recipe for crab cakes, combining blue crab with chopped hard-boiled eggs and plenty of melted butter, comes from Aunt Marion. She's not my Aunt Marion; she's the great-aunt of my catering chef, Chris Field. Chris used to cook these crab cakes in the family restaurant in Pennsylvania, where they were offered either broiled or "triple breaded" and fried.

These cakes are light, creamy, and delicate inside, with a beautiful, crisp, golden crust. See "How to Deep-Fry" on page 27.

1 pound lump blue crabmeat, drained and picked clean of shell

½ pound unsalted butter, melted and slightly cooled

¼ cup chopped parsley

3 tablespoons thinly sliced chives

2 hard-boiled eggs, finely chopped

1 teaspoon kosher salt

¼ teaspoon freshly ground black pepper

1½ cups fresh bread crumbs (see page 7)

1 cup all-purpose flour

2 large eggs, lightly beaten with 2 tablespoons water

2½ cups dried bread crumbs (see page 7)

Peanut or canola oil, as needed for frying

Really Good Tartar Sauce (page 128) or Spicy Corn Tartar Sauce (page 129)

Put the crabmeat in a large bowl and add the butter, parsley, chives, eggs, salt, and pepper. Mix with a rubber spatula until everything is combined. Add the fresh bread crumbs and blend very well with the spatula until you have a coherent mixture.

Divide the crab mixture firmly into 10 portions. (A packed 2-ounce ice cream scoop works well.) Flatten the mounds into patties, about 2¾ inches wide by ½ inch thick. Put the patties on a large plate, cover with plastic wrap, and refrigerate for 30 minutes or longer.

When you are ready to fry the crab cakes, preheat the oven to 200°F and set out 3 shallow containers. Put the flour in one container, the egg wash in the second, and the dried bread crumbs in the third. Dredge one of the patties on all sides in the flour, then drop it into the egg wash. Turn the patty to coat all sides with egg wash, then drop it into the bread crumbs. Turn the patty to coat evenly and thoroughly with the crumbs. Then shake off excess crumbs and place the patty on a large plate. Continue until all the patties are breaded.

Clip a deep-frying thermometer to a straight-sided pot. Fill the pot with at least 2 inches of oil and heat to 350°F, checking the temperature on the thermometer. Add as many crab cakes as will comfortably fit and fry, turning a few times with a slotted spoon, until golden brown on all sides and hot through, about 6 minutes total cooking time.

Remove the crab cakes with a slotted spoon, drain on paper towels, and keep warm in the oven while you finish frying the remaining crab cakes.

Transfer the crab cakes to plates, serving 2 per person, and accompany with tartar sauce.

# How to Deep-Fry

I prefer peanut, grapeseed, or canola oil for deep-frying because of their high smoke points and clean, neutral flavors. Some people buy an electric deep-fat fryer, but I use a wok or a heavy, straight-sided pot. A frying thermometer is the most important element for successful deep-frying, especially one that clips onto the side of the pot.

Add 1 to 3 inches of oil to the pot, but not more than halfway because the hot oil will bubble up when food is added.

Heat the oil to 350°F. Maintaining a consistent temperature is crucial. Once the crab cakes are added, the temperature of the oil will fluctuate. When you add crab cakes to the oil they will lower the temperature, or the oil may get hotter the longer it is on the burner. Use your thermometer to check the temperature of the oil before you start frying and keep checking throughout the frying process, adjusting the heat of the burner up or down to keep the temperature consistent. The other rule is not to add too many crab cakes to the oil as that will also lower the oil's temperature.

A spider (a Chinese mesh strainer on a bamboo handle) or a skimmer (a small, flat, wire-mesh basket on the end of a long handle) is the perfect tool for removing foods from hot oil.

Frying is potentially dangerous. Work carefully and keep a box of salt or baking soda on hand, or a large lid to smother a small fire. It's a good idea to have a working fire extinguisher nearby.

# JAZZ FEST CRAB AND CRAYFISH CAKES

*Makes 8 large crab cakes*

This recipe from Susan Spicer, chef-owner of Bayona, celebrates the New Orleans Jazz and Heritage Festival, which takes place every year at the end of April. Susan sometimes can't resist the urge to gild the lily and add succulent crayfish tails to her Louisiana blue crab cakes. But if you prefer, make these crab cakes with a pound of crabmeat and omit the crayfish.

Susan serves these cakes with a creamy beurre blanc made with Crystal brand hot sauce, but any spicy remoulade or tartar sauce works well.

- 2 tablespoons unsalted butter
- 1 small yellow onion, peeled and finely chopped (about ¾ cup)
- 1 celery stalk, finely chopped
- ½ red bell pepper, seeded and finely chopped (about ½ cup)
- 1 small jalapeño pepper, seeded and minced (1 tablespoon)
- ½ cup finely chopped scallions, green and white parts, plus 2 tablespoons more for garnish
- ¼ teaspoon minced garlic
- ½ pound lump blue crabmeat, drained and picked clean of shell
- ½ pound cooked crayfish tails, coarsely chopped
- ¾ cup mayonnaise
- 3 tablespoons fresh lemon juice
- 1 tablespoon plus 1 teaspoon grated lemon zest
- 1 tablespoon Dijon mustard
- ½ cup dried bread crumbs (see page 7), plus about 2 cups more for dredging
- Kosher salt
- Freshly ground black pepper
- Hot sauce, such as Tabasco
- ¼ cup olive oil, for frying
- Spicy Remoulade (page 134) or Spicy Corn Tartar Sauce (page 129)

Heat the butter in a large skillet over medium heat and sweat the onion, celery, bell pepper, and jalapeño for about 3 minutes, stirring. Add the ½ cup scallions, garlic, crabmeat, and crayfish, and stir to mix. Cook for 3 to 5 minutes, then scrape the mixture into a large bowl, carefully checking again for bits of shell. Let the mixture cool in the refrigerator for about 20 minutes. If you notice that liquid has collected in the bowl while the vegetables and seafood were cooling, drain it off first. Then stir in the mayonnaise, lemon juice and zest, mustard, and ½ cup of the bread crumbs, and stir with a rubber spatula to mix. Season to taste with salt, pepper, and hot sauce. Form the mixture into 8 cakes. Pour the remaining 2 cups bread crumbs into a shallow container and dredge the cakes in the crumbs. If you have time, cover the crab cakes with plastic wrap and refrigerate for 30 minutes or more.

When you are ready to cook the crab cakes, place 2 large nonstick skillets over medium heat and pour 2 tablespoons olive oil into each pan. Add 4 cakes to each pan and fry until golden brown on both sides and hot through, turning once with a spatula, 4 to 5 minutes per side. The internal temperature of a crab cake should read 155°F on an instant-read thermometer.

Transfer the crab cakes to plates, serving 2 to each person. Sprinkle with the reserved scallions, and serve with remoulade or tartar sauce.

★

# TIDEWATER CRAB CAKES WITH SMITHFIELD HAM

*Makes 8 large crab cakes*

My friend Chris Schlesinger, who contributed this recipe, owns the East Coast Grill in Cambridge, Massachusetts. Chris also cowrote, with John Willoughby, one of my favorite cookbooks of all time, *The Thrill of the Grill*.

To make the corn-bread crumbs, use your favorite corn-bread recipe.

⅓ cup finely diced Smithfield ham, or substitute any country ham or prosciutto

1 pound lump blue crabmeat, drained and picked clean of shell

½ cup corn-bread crumbs

2 large eggs

¼ cup heavy cream

2 tablespoons whole mustard seeds

1 tablespoon chopped fresh sage

7 dashes of Tabasco

¼ teaspoon kosher salt

¼ teaspoon freshly ground black pepper

½ cup all-purpose flour

4 tablespoons (½ stick) unsalted butter

Really Good Tartar Sauce (page 128)

Put a small skillet over medium heat, add the ham, sauté for a few minutes, then set aside to cool.

In a large bowl, combine the crabmeat and corn-bread crumbs. In another bowl, whisk the eggs with the cream, then pour it over the crabmeat. Add the ham, mustard seeds, sage, Tabasco, salt, and pepper. Mix everything together well and form into 8 cakes, about 3 inches in diameter and ¾ inch thick.

Put the flour in a shallow container. Dredge the cakes lightly in the flour, on both sides, patting off excess, and set them on a large plate.

Put 2 large nonstick skillets over medium-high heat and add 2 tablespoons butter to each pan. When the butter is hot, add 4 cakes to each pan, turning the heat down to medium. Fry the cakes until golden brown and heated through, turning once with a spatula to brown both sides, 3 to 4 minutes per side. The internal temperature of a crab cake should read 155°F on an instant-read thermometer.

Remove the crab cakes from the pans, drain on paper towels if needed, and transfer to plates, serving 2 per person. Serve immediately, with tartar sauce on the side.

# MARK BITTMAN'S VERY CRABBY CRAB CAKES

*Makes 8 large crab cakes*

Mark has long been one of my favorite food writers. His minimalist approach is perfect for the harried and time-sensitive home cook. These crab cakes are easy to make and full of crab flavor. You can use purchased mayo here, but Mark prefers homemade.

1 pound fresh lump crabmeat, drained and picked clean of shell

1 large egg

1/4 cup minced red bell pepper

1/2 cup minced scallions, green and white parts

1/4 cup mayonnaise

1 tablespoon Dijon mustard

Kosher salt

Freshly ground black pepper

2 tablespoons dried bread crumbs (see page 7), as needed

About 1 cup all-purpose flour, for dredging

1 teaspoon curry powder (optional)

2 tablespoons peanut, olive, or vegetable oil

2 tablespoons unsalted butter

4 lemon wedges

In a large bowl, mix together the crabmeat, egg, bell pepper, scallions, mayonnaise, and mustard. Season with 1/4 teaspoon salt and 1/4 teaspoon pepper, and stir in the bread crumbs. If you have time, cover the bowl with plastic wrap and chill the crab cake mixture for 30 minutes or more.

When you are ready to cook the crab cakes, put the flour in a shallow container and season it to taste with salt, pepper, and the curry powder, if using. Remove the crab mixture from the refrigerator and shape it into 8 cakes. The crab cakes will be soft. If you have trouble forming cakes, add a little more bread crumbs.

Place 2 large nonstick skillets over medium-high heat for 2 or 3 minutes. Add 1 table spoon oil and 1 tablespoon butter to each pan and heat until the butter foam subsides. Dredge the cakes in the flour and cook 4 cakes in each pan, lowering the heat to medium and gently turning once with a spatula, until golden brown on both sides, 4 to 5 minutes per side. The internal temperature of a crab cake should read 155°F on an instant-read thermometer.

Transfer the crab cakes to plates, serving 2 per person, and accompany with lemon wedges.

# THIERRY'S DUNGENESS CRAB CAKES

*Makes 4 large crab cakes*

Thierry Rautureau, a chef transplanted from the west coast of France, owns one of Seattle's most admired restaurants, Rover's, in Madison Valley. Thierry's indignant response to his first taste of my classic Etta's cakes—"These are bread cakes not crab cakes"—inspired his take on the classic American crab cake.

You will need 4 ring molds for this recipe, 2 to 2½ inches in diameter and a few inches deep. See page 117.

³⁄₄ pound Dungeness crabmeat, drained, picked clean of shell, and lightly squeezed if wet (see page 5)

2 teaspoons minced garlic

2 tablespoons finely chopped shallots

2 tablespoons thinly sliced chives

1 tablespoon finely chopped basil

Freshly ground black pepper

½ cup dried bread crumbs (see page 7)

2 large egg yolks, lightly beaten with 1 tablespoon water

2 tablespoons olive oil

Clam Aioli (page 138)

1 tablespoon thinly sliced chives

To make the crab cakes, put the crabmeat on a cutting board and chop it into small pieces. No piece of crab should be larger than the size of a pea. (It's important to chop the crab so you get a nice tight pack in the mold without air spaces.) Transfer the crabmeat to a bowl and add the garlic, shallots, chives, basil, and a little ground pepper to taste.

Set 4 ring molds on a work surface. Divide the crab mixture among the molds, packing the crab as tightly as you can into each mold with your fingers or the back of a spoon. Put the

bread crumbs on a plate. Leaving the crabmeat in the mold, use a spoon to generously spread an even layer of egg wash on top of the crabmeat. Turn the mold upside down (egg-washed side down) onto the plate of bread crumbs. If the crabmeat is not even with the edge of the mold on both sides, push down on the crabmeat with your fingers so the egg-washed side makes contact with the bread crumbs. Generously spoon the egg wash over the unbreaded side of the mold, and turn the mold upside down again to bread-crumb the other side, pushing down on the crabmeat if needed to make contact with the crumbs. Both the top and bottom sides of the crabmeat in the mold should be evenly covered with a layer of egg wash and crumbs. Set the mold aside and repeat with the remaining molds.

Set a large nonstick skillet over medium-high heat and add the oil. When the skillet is hot, pick up a mold and place in the pan, then use your fingers to carefully push the crab cake out of the mold, removing the mold from the pan. Repeat with the remaining molds. Cook the crab cakes until browned on the first side, about 1 minute, then very carefully turn them over, using a spatula, and brown the second side, about a minute more.

Set out 4 plates and set a crab cake on each plate. Ladle some of the Clam Aioli around each crab cake, sprinkle with chives, and serve.

# PEEKYTOE MAINE CRAB CAKES

*Makes 8 large crab cakes*

This recipe is from Susan Regis, the gregarious chef of Upstairs on the Square in Cambridge, Massachusetts. I met Susan when she was chef at Biba in Boston, and have been inspired ever since by her instinct for unusual flavor combinations that spark my imagination and my palate.

Susan likes to make a spicy, citrusy, golden yellow sauce with aji Amarillo chile peppers to serve with her Peekytoe cakes. Aji Amarillo yellow pepper sauce is available in Latino markets, but if you can't find it, Green Cocktail Sauce makes a light and tangy accompaniment to these rich cakes.

Peekytoe, or Jonah crab, is very similar in texture to Dungeness crab.

1 large egg yolk

1 tablespoon fresh lemon juice

1 tablespoon dry mustard, such as Coleman's, mixed with 2 teaspoons water to form a slurry

1/2 teaspoon minced garlic

3/4 cup peanut or canola oil

2 1/2 teaspoons kosher salt or to taste

3 tablespoons unsalted butter

1 cup finely chopped onion, preferably a sweet onion like Spanish or Walla Walla

3 tablespoons seeded and minced jalapeño pepper, preferably red

1 pound Peekytoe crabmeat, drained and picked clean of shell

3/4 cup roughly chopped fresh cilantro

1/2 cup celery leaves, tender inner leaves only, coarsely chopped

1/2 cup thinly sliced scallions

2 teaspoons grated lemon zest

1/2 cup panko (see page 10), plus 2 cups more for dredging

4 cilantro sprigs

4 lemon wedges

Aji Amarillo Sauce (page 137) or Green Cocktail Sauce (page 127)

To make the aioli for the crab cakes, put the egg yolk and lemon juice in a bowl and whisk together well. Add the mustard and garlic. Slowly add the oil in a thin stream while whisking constantly until the mixture emulsifies. Season with ½ teaspoon of the salt. (You could also make the aioli in a medium or mini food processor or a blender, combining the yolk, lemon juice, mustard, and garlic first, then adding the oil slowly with the machine running.) Set the aioli aside, refrigerated.

Place a large skillet over medium heat and add the butter. When the butter is melted, add the onion and cook gently, stirring, until translucent, 3 to 4 minutes. Add the jalapeño and cook for another minute. Remove the pan from the heat and allow to cool. Transfer the onion mixture to a large bowl and add the crabmeat, cilantro, celery leaves, scallions, and lemon zest. Season with the remaining 2 teaspoons salt. Mix gently with a rubber spatula until combined, then fold in the reserved aioli and the ½ cup panko.

Divide the crab mixture into 8 mounds and shape them into 8 flattened patties, about ¾ inch thick. Pour the 2 cups panko in a shallow container. Lightly dredge or sprinkle the patties on both sides with some of the panko.

Put 2 large nonstick skillets over medium heat, without adding any fat. When the skillets are hot, add 4 patties to each of the dry pans. Cook until golden brown on both sides and heated through, turning once with a spatula, about 4 minutes per side. The internal temperature of a crab cake should read 155°F on an instant-read thermometer.

Transfer the crab cakes to plates, serving 2 to each person. Garnish each plate with a sprig of cilantro and a lemon wedge, and serve with the Aji Amarillo Sauce or Green Cocktail Sauce.

# BEER BATTER CRAB FRITTERS

*Makes 24 to 26 fritters, 4 to 6 servings*

Emeril Lagasse has made the home fryer popular again, and it's great fun to get it out in the middle of a cocktail party and cook these fritters right in front of people. I steal the little paper cone cups next to the water cooler at work and fill each one with a scoop of fritters and a little remoulade drizzled right on top.

Use a light, lager-style beer for the batter, not a dark beer, which would overpower the flavor of the crab.

See "How to Deep-Fry," page 27.

2/3 cup all-purpose flour

1 teaspoon smoked or sweet paprika

1 teaspoon kosher salt

1/4 teaspoon freshly ground black pepper

1/4 teaspoon cayenne

1/4 cup minced red bell pepper

2 scallions, finely chopped, white and green parts

1/3 cup plus 1 tablespoon beer

1 large egg, separated

1 1/2 teaspoons unsalted butter, melted

1/2 pound crabmeat, drained, picked clean of shell, and lightly squeezed if wet (see page 5)

Peanut or canola oil, as needed for frying

Spicy Remoulade (page 134)

4 to 6 lemon wedges

In a bowl, mix together the flour, paprika, salt, pepper, and cayenne. Add the bell pepper, scallions, beer, egg yolk, and butter. Using a rubber spatula, fold in the crabmeat. In another bowl, using an electric mixer, whip the egg white to soft peaks. Gently but thoroughly fold the egg white into the fritter mixture.

Preheat the oven to 200°F. Fill a straight-sided pot with at least 2 inches of oil and heat to 350°F, checking the temperature with a frying thermometer. Drop scant tablespoons of batter into the hot oil, adding as many as fit comfortably. Fry the fritters until golden brown, puffy, and cooked through, turning a few times with a slotted spoon, about 4 minutes total cooking time. Before you remove the fritters from the oil, pull one out and cut it open to make sure the dough is cooked through. Remove the fritters from the oil with a slotted spoon, drain on paper towels, and keep warm in the oven while you fry the remaining batter. You should get 24 to 26 small fritters.

Transfer the fritters to plates and serve hot with the Spicy Remoulade and lemon wedges.

★

# GLOBAL/
# NEW WAVE
# CRAB
# CAKES

# TEMPURA CRAB CAKES WITH SHREDDED NORI

*Makes 16 small crab cakes, 4 servings*

Crisp tempura batter and the salty, ocean tang of nori seaweed give a Japanese flavor to these cakes. Don't be stingy with the batter as you slip them into the oil because it makes for great crispy strands curling off each cake. See "How to Deep-Fry," page 27.

Yuzu juice, often sold in small plastic bottles, is made from a sour Japanese citrus fruit. It has a unique fruity aroma, but you can substitute fresh lime juice. Shiso, an aromatic green leaf in the mint and basil family, is often used as a garnish in sushi bars. There is no substitute for shiso, but you can omit it if you can't find it, or add a tablespoon of thinly sliced chives instead. Nori is roasted and dried seaweed often used for making sushi. Paper-thin sheets of nori are sold stacked in cellophane bags. Yuzu, shiso, and nori are available in specialty Asian markets or Japanese fish markets. Nori can often be found in supermarkets as well.

3 sheets nori, about 7 inches by 8 inches

½ pound crabmeat, drained, picked clean of shell, and lightly squeezed if wet (see page 5)

6 tablespoons mayonnaise

5 shiso leaves, cut in half and thinly shredded

1 teaspoon yuzu juice or fresh lime juice

¼ teaspoon cayenne

Pinch of kosher salt

6 tablespoons panko (see page 10)

Peanut or canola oil, as needed for frying

Ice cubes

2 cups club soda

1¾ cups all-purpose flour

Sake Sauce (page 140)

Preheat the oven to 200°F.

Using scissors, cut the sheets of nori into lengthwise strips, about 1 inch wide. Then cut the strips crosswise into thin shreds, about ⅛ inch thick. Put the shreds on a plate and set aside.

In a large bowl, mix the crabmeat with the mayonnaise, shiso, yuzu, cayenne, and salt. Using a rubber spatula, fold in the panko and combine thoroughly. Divide the mixture into 16 small mounds and shape each mound into a ball. Roll each ball in the shredded nori, covering it as evenly as possible. Set the crab cakes aside on a large plate.

Clip a deep-frying thermometer to a straight sided pot. Fill the pot with at least 2 inches of oil and heat to 350°F, checking the temperature on the thermometer.

Meanwhile, make the tempura batter. Add a few ice cubes to the club soda and allow it to chill for a few minutes. Remove the ice cubes, then whisk the iced club soda with the flour in a bowl. Put the bowl of tempura batter in another bowl of ice water and set it by the stove.

Drop a crab cake into the tempura batter, then remove it with a soup spoon, making sure that it is generously coated on all sides with batter. Drop as many battered cakes at a time into the oil as will fit comfortably. Fry the crab cakes until golden and cooked through, 4 to 5 minutes, turning occasionally with a slotted spoon or spider. Remove the crab cakes from the oil, drain on paper towels, and keep warm in the oven while you finish frying the rest of the crab cakes. (You may need to skim out the fried batter debris with a slotted spoon or spider in between frying batches of cakes.)

Transfer the crab cakes to plates and serve with ramekins of Sake Sauce.

# COCONUT MILK CRAB CAKES WITH LIME ZEST

*Makes 8 large crab cakes*

These crab cakes have a surprisingly distinct coconut flavor from the coconut milk reduction.

1 can (13.5 ounces) coconut milk, unsweetened

1 tablespoon grated lime zest

1 pound crabmeat, drained, picked clean of shell, and lightly squeezed if wet (see page 5)

3 scallions, thinly sliced, green and white parts

1 tablespoon finely chopped fresh cilantro

1 tablespoon fresh lime juice

¼ teaspoon kosher salt

¼ teaspoon freshly ground black pepper

1 cup panko, plus 2 cups more for dredging (see page 10)

2 large egg whites

Peanut or canola oil for frying

Sweet chile sauce (see page 11)

4 lime wedges

Combine the coconut milk and lime zest in a small saucepan and bring to a simmer over medium heat. Continue to simmer until the milk is reduced by about one-third, adjusting the heat as necessary. (You should have about ¾ cup reduced coconut milk.) Transfer the coconut milk to a large bowl and refrigerate until cold.

When the coconut milk is cold, add the crabmeat, scallions, cilantro, lime juice, salt, and pepper, stirring to combine. Stir in the 1 cup panko. In the bowl of an electric mixer, whip the egg whites to soft peaks. Using a rubber spatula, fold the egg whites into the crab mixture gently but thoroughly.

Divide the mixture into 8 portions, then flatten into patties. Pour the remaining 2 cups panko into a shallow container. Dredge the patties in the panko. If time permits, you can cover and chill the cakes for 30 minutes or more.

When ready to fry the crab cakes, place 2 large nonstick skillets over medium-high heat, and pour in enough oil to coat the bottoms of the pans about ⅛ inch deep. When the oil is hot, shake off any excess panko from the patties, add 4 patties to each pan, and reduce the heat to medium. Fry until the crab cakes are golden brown and heated through, turning once with a spatula to brown both sides, 3 to 4 minutes per side. The internal temperature of a crab cake should read 155°F on an instant-read thermometer. Remove the crab cakes from the pans and drain on paper towels.

Transfer the crab cakes to plates, serving 2 to each person, accompanied by ramekins of sweet chile sauce and lime wedges.

★

# PESTO RISOTTO CRAB CAKES

Because these risotto cakes are dredged in a mixture of Parmesan and dried bread crumbs, they get a beautiful golden crust when panfried. Try them as a first course before serving something simple and dramatic like a whole roasted or grilled fish.

1 tablespoon pine nuts

1½ cups loosely packed fresh basil, washed and dried

1 tablespoon plus 1 teaspoon fresh lemon juice

1½ teaspoons grated lemon zest

1 teaspoon minced garlic

2 tablespoons extra virgin olive oil

2 cups dry white wine

2 cups water

1 tablespoon plus 1 teaspoon unsalted butter

½ cup finely chopped onion

½ cup Arborio rice

½ pound crabmeat, drained, picked clean of shell, and lightly squeezed if wet (see page 5)

⅔ plus ¾ cup grated Parmesan

2 large eggs, lightly beaten

½ teaspoon kosher salt

½ teaspoon freshly ground black pepper

¾ cup dried bread crumbs (see page 7)

Olive oil, as needed for frying

Fresh Tomato Relish (page 131)

To make the pesto, put the pine nuts in a small, heavy skillet and toast over medium heat for a few minutes, stirring, until they are lightly browned. Remove from the heat and allow to cool slightly. Put the basil, pine nuts, lemon juice and zest, and garlic in the bowl of a food processor or a blender and process until smooth. Slowly add the olive oil through the feed tube and process until well combined. Transfer to a bowl and set aside.

To make the risotto, combine the wine and water in a small saucepan and heat to a simmer. Melt the butter in a sauté pan over medium-high heat. Add the onion and cook until light golden brown, stirring as needed. Add the rice and stir a few minutes. Start adding the simmering liquid, a small ladle at a time, bringing the risotto to a simmer and stirring occasionally until most of the liquid is absorbed. Continue adding the simmering liquid, lowering the heat as needed and stirring occasionally. As soon as the rice is tender, after about 20 minutes, stop adding liquid. (You may not need all of the wine-water mixture.) If the rice is soupy, raise the heat slightly to boil away most of the moisture. Remove the risotto from the heat, transfer to a bowl, and place in the refrigerator to cool to room temperature. When the risotto has cooled, stir in the pesto, crabmeat, the ⅔ cup Parmesan, eggs, salt, and pepper. Form the risotto into 12 flattened cakes, about ¼ cup each.

To make the dredging mixture, combine the bread crumbs and the ¾ cup Parmesan in a shallow pan. Dredge the crab cakes on both sides, patting off excess.

Film the bottoms of 2 large nonstick or cast-iron skillets with olive oil about ⅛ inch deep and heat over medium-high heat. When the oil is hot, add as many crab cakes as will fit comfortably in the pans. Fry the crab cakes, lowering the heat as needed, until golden on both sides, 4 to 5 minutes total cooking time. (If you need to fry the cakes in batches, keep the finished cakes warm in a 200°F oven.) The internal temperature of a crab cake should read 155°F on an instant-read thermometer.

Transfer the cakes to 4 plates, garnish each serving with a generous spoonful of Fresh Tomato Relish, and serve immediately.

★

# HERBES DE PROVENCE CRAB CAKES

*Makes 8 large crab cakes*

I usually make my own herb mixes, but herbes de Provence is a perfect blend and has always caught my fancy, whether I'm panfrying oysters in an herbes de Provence flour, making an herbes de Provence mustard for glazing barbecued chicken, or creating these crab cakes.

This classic dried-herb blend from Provence typically contains chervil, marjoram, tarragon, basil, thyme, and lavender. It's available in the spice section of well-stocked supermarkets as well as specialty stores.

2 large egg yolks

2 tablespoons Dijon mustard

2 tablespoons good-quality red wine vinegar

2 tablespoons plus 1 teaspoon herbes de Provence (1 teaspoon crushed in a mortar and pestle or with a heavy rolling pin)

¼ teaspoon kosher salt

½ teaspoon freshly ground black pepper

½ cup extra virgin olive oil

1 pound crabmeat, drained, picked clean of shell, and lightly squeezed if wet (see page 5)

2 tablespoons dried bread crumbs (see page 7)

1 cup all-purpose flour

About 4 tablespoons unsalted butter

Fresh Tomato Relish (page 131) or Red Pepper Rouille (page 143)

Put the egg yolks, mustard, red wine vinegar, 1 teaspoon crushed herbes de Provence, the salt, and pepper in the bowl of a food processor or a blender. With the machine running, gradually add the oil until the mixture emulsifies. Transfer the mayonnaise to a bowl. Add the crabmeat and stir to combine with the mayonnaise. Sprinkle the bread crumbs into the bowl, then gently mix with a rubber spatula. Divide the mixture into 8 mounds and form into patties about 3 inches wide by ⅔ inch thick. (The patties will be soft.) Put the patties on a large plate, cover with plastic wrap, and chill for an hour or longer.

In a shallow container, combine the flour with the 2 tablespoons herbes de Provence. Dredge the patties on both sides with the flour mixture, patting off excess flour.

Heat 2 large nonstick skillets over medium heat. Add about 2 tablespoons butter to each pan. When the butter melts, add 4 patties to each pan. Fry slowly until golden on both sides and hot through, turning once with a spatula, 4 to 5 minutes per side. The internal temperature of a crab cake should read 155°F on an instant-read thermometer.

Transfer the crab cakes to plates, serving 2 to each person. Spoon some Fresh Tomato Relish or Red Pepper Rouille next to the crab cakes on each plate and serve.

# VIETNAMESE CRAB SHRIMP TOASTS

*Makes 14 toasts, 4 to 6 appetizer servings*

These will remind you of those oh-so-delicious shrimp toasts you get right off a dim sum cart.

When you puree shrimp or scallops or lobster like this, you get a pasty mixture that takes well to other flavors and cooks up with a satisfying sausage-like texture.

6 ounces peeled raw shrimp

6 ounces crabmeat, drained, picked clean of shell, and lightly squeezed if wet (see page 5)

1 tablespoon picked cilantro leaves

1 teaspoon Vietnamese or Thai fish sauce

1 teaspoon minced shallots

14 slices French baguette, cut crosswise, each slice about ½ inch thick and 2¾ inches long

Peanut or canola oil

Lime Dipping Sauce (page 141) or sweet chile sauce (see page 11)

4 to 6 lime wedges

Put the shrimp in the bowl of a food processor and process until as smooth as possible. Add the crabmeat, cilantro, fish sauce, and shallots, and pulse until well combined. Transfer to a bowl and use a rubber spatula to fold the mixture together several times.

Place a heaping tablespoon of the crab mixture on top of one of the baguette slices and use a butter knife to spread it in an even layer to the edges of the bread. Repeat with the remaining baguette slices, using up all of the crab mixture.

Preheat the oven to 200°F.

Heat about ¼ inch of oil in a large nonstick or cast-iron skillet over medium-high heat. When the oil is hot (a cube of bread will turn golden within 30 seconds), add as many toasts as will comfortably fit in the pan, crab side down. Fry until the crab mixture is golden brown, 1 to 2 minutes. Using metal tongs, turn the toasts over to fry the undersides to a light golden brown, less than 1 minute. Remove the toasts from the pan, drain on paper towels, and keep warm in the oven. Continue until all the toasts are fried.

Cut the toasts on the diagonal and serve immediately with ramekins of Lime Dipping Sauce or sweet chile sauce and lime wedges.

★

# CRAB FOO YUNG

*Makes 8, 4 servings*

Here's my version of an old-fashioned Chinese-American classic, egg foo yung. Simply squeeze a wedge of lemon over the tops of these delicately flavored crab patties or get feisty with some chili paste or Tabasco sauce.

4 large eggs

2 teaspoons soy sauce

2 teaspoons mirin (sweet cooking rice wine, such as Kikkoman)

½ teaspoon Tabasco or to taste

¾ pound crabmeat, drained, picked clean of shell, and lightly squeezed if wet (see page 5)

1 cup sliced shiitake mushrooms, stems removed

1 cup mung bean sprouts

¼ cup minced celery, preferably the tender inner stems and a few leaves

¼ cup thinly sliced scallions, white and green parts

About 6 tablespoons peanut or canola oil, as needed

4 lemon wedges

Tabasco or Chinese hot chili paste

Whisk the eggs with the soy sauce, mirin, and Tabasco in a large bowl until slightly foamy. Stir in the crabmeat, mushrooms, sprouts, celery, and scallions. Heat 2 large nonstick skillets over medium-high heat with about 3 tablespoons oil in each one. When the oil is hot, ladle as many patties as will fit into each pan (3 or 4) using a 4-ounce ladle or a ½-cup measuring cup. Fry the patties until golden brown on both sides and cooked through, about 4 minutes total, turning the heat down as needed. Use a spatula to turn the patties from side to side a few times while they're cooking so they don't get too dark. Remove the patties from the pan, and drain on paper towels. If you can't fit all the patties in the pans at once and need to fry them in batches, keep the finished patties warm in a 200°F oven while you wipe out the pan with a paper towel, add more oil, and continue to fry the remaining patties. You should get about 8 crab foo yung.

Serve with lemon wedges and Tabasco or hot chili paste.

# POBLANO CRAB RELLENOS

*Makes 6 servings*

These roasted poblano peppers, stuffed with fresh crabmeat and queso fresco, dredged in fragrant masa harina and panfried, make a great first course, or, as a dinner entrée, serve them with refried black beans and rice.

Masa harina is a flour made from dried and ground masa, which is the corn dough used for making tortillas. Queso fresco is a white, somewhat salty, fresh Mexican cheese. Both are available in Latino markets and many supermarkets.

Poblano peppers are usually only mild to medium hot, but the heat in individual chiles can vary. If you like, you can reduce the amount of chipotle peppers in the crab filling to make the dish less spicy.

½ pound crabmeat, drained, picked clean of shell, lightly squeezed if wet (see page 5)

¾ cup grated queso fresco or Jack cheese

¼ cup fresh bread crumbs (see page 7)

2 tablespoons minced scallions, white and green parts

1 tablespoon plus 1 teaspoon chopped fresh cilantro

1 tablespoon plus 1 teaspoon fresh lime juice

1 to 3 teaspoons pureed canned chipotle peppers in adobo, to taste (see page 8)

6 poblano peppers, roasted, peeled, split open, and seeded (see page 62), leaving the stems on

3 large egg whites

1½ cups all-purpose flour

1½ cups masa harina

½ teaspoon kosher salt

½ teaspoon paprika

Peanut or canola oil, as needed for frying

Sour cream

Tomato-Avocado Salsa (page 135)

Preheat the oven to 375°F.

In a bowl, combine the crabmeat, cheese, bread crumbs, scallions, cilantro, lime juice, and chipotle. Lay the poblano peppers out on a work surface. Divide the filling between the peppers, enclosing the filling completely.

In the bowl of an electric mixer, whip the egg whites until they are very thick and foamy. Set aside. Set out 1 large plate and 2 shallow containers (such as 9- by 13-inch Pyrex baking pans). Spread the flour on the plate, leave one container empty, and combine the masa harina with the salt and paprika in the third container. Dredge each pepper lightly in the flour, then

place them in a single layer in the empty container. When all the peppers are floured, pour the egg whites over them. Using your hands, smooth the egg whites as evenly as possible over both sides of each pepper, then pick the pepper up and lay it in the pan of masa. When all the peppers are in a single layer in the masa, wash and dry your hands, then dredge the peppers with masa on both sides.

Put 2 large nonstick or cast-iron skillets over medium-high heat and pour in enough oil to coat the bottoms about ¼ inch deep. When the oil is hot, add 3 peppers to each pan. Fry until golden on the first side, about 3 minutes, turning the heat down to medium as needed. Turn with a spatula and fry the other side for about 2 minutes. Use a slotted spoon to transfer the peppers to a baking sheet and bake until heated through, about 8 minutes.

Transfer the peppers to 6 plates and serve with the sour cream and Tomato-Avocado Salsa.

★

# Roasted and Peeled Peppers

Place the peppers directly over the open flame of a gas burner, turning them with tongs until the skins are blackened, blistered, and charred all over. Or place the peppers on a baking sheet under a hot broiler, turning as needed.

Remove to a bowl, cover tightly with plastic wrap, and allow the peppers to sweat for about 10 minutes to loosen the skins. Take the peppers out of the bowl and scrape away all the skin with a paring knife or pull it off using your fingers. Core out the stems and use your knife to split the peppers open. Remove and discard the seeds and veins, then slice or chop the peppers as needed.

For the Poblano Crab Rellenos, carefully split open a roasted and peeled chile on one side, leaving the stem attached. Reach inside the chile and remove and discard as much of the seeds and veins as possible, without disturbing the basic shape of the pepper.

# COCONUT-CRUSTED CRAB CAKES

*Makes 8 large crab cakes*

These easy-to-make cakes feature the harmonious flavors of fresh ginger, coconut, and crab. You can find unsweetened shredded coconut in the bulk section of some supermarkets and in natural food stores. Don't use the sweetened shredded coconut found in the supermarket baking aisle.

1 pound crabmeat, drained, picked clean of shell, lightly squeezed if wet (see page 5)

1 cup mayonnaise

½ cup thinly sliced scallions, green and white parts

¼ cup finely diced red bell pepper

2 teaspoons peeled and grated fresh ginger

½ teaspoon kosher salt

½ teaspoon freshly ground black pepper

½ cup unsweetened shredded coconut, plus 1 cup more for dredging

½ cup panko (see page 10), plus 1 cup more for dredging

About 6 tablespoons peanut or canola oil

Sweet chile sauce (see page 11)

4 lime wedges

Put the crabmeat in a large bowl and add the mayonnaise, scallions, bell pepper, ginger, salt, and pepper, and gently combine, using a rubber spatula. Add the ½ cup coconut and ½ cup panko and gently fold in. Divide the mixture into 8 mounds and form into patties about 3 inches in diameter and ¾ inch thick. Put the patties on a large plate, cover with plastic wrap, and refrigerate 30 minutes or longer.

When you are ready to fry the crab cakes, combine the remaining 1 cup coconut and 1 cup panko in a shallow container. Lightly dredge the patties in the crumbs, shaking off any excess. Put 2 large nonstick skillets over medium-high heat. Add about 3 tablespoons oil to each pan. When the pans are hot, place 4 patties in each pan. Turn the heat down to medium and fry the cakes until golden and heated through, turning once with a spatula to brown both sides, about 4 minutes per side. The internal temperature of a crab cake should read 155°F on an instant-read thermometer.

Transfer the crab cakes to plates, serving 2 to each person, accompanied by ramekins of sweet chile sauce and lime wedges.

★

# CRAB AND SCALLOP CAKES STEAMED IN BANANA LEAVES

*Makes 4 servings as an appetizer*

Banana leaves are commonly used in Southeast Asia as wrappers for steamed or grilled fish, chicken, or rice. The leaves protect the food from the heat and seal in the juices, and impart a grassy aroma to the dish, a little like green tea. You'll find banana leaves in sealed plastic bags in the freezer section of Asian markets.

For steaming, a multitiered Chinese bamboo steamer with two steamer baskets works best. Set the bamboo steamer over a wok or a large saucepan partially filled with boiling water. If you don't have a multitiered steamer, divide the packets between two pots with steamer baskets.

You can make these ahead, chill them, and reheat the filled banana leaves in the steamer baskets for about 5 minutes or pop them on a hot grill for a nice charred and smoky flavor.

1 tablespoon peanut or canola oil

1 cup sliced shiitake mushrooms, stems removed

½ pound sea scallops

½ pound crabmeat, drained, picked clean of shell, and lightly squeezed if wet (see page 5)

3 tablespoons thinly sliced chives

1 tablespoon plus 1 teaspoon mirin

¼ teaspoon ground star anise (see page 11)

¼ teaspoon sambal (see page 10)

¼ teaspoon kosher salt

1 package banana leaves, thawed if frozen

Sweet chile sauce (see page 11)

4 lime wedges

Heat the oil in a skillet over medium-high heat. Add the shiitakes and sauté, stirring as needed, until cooked through and slightly crisp around the edges, 5 to 7 minutes. Remove from the heat and allow to cool.

Place the scallops in the bowl of a food processor and puree until smooth. Transfer to a bowl and, using a rubber spatula, fold in the shiitakes, crabmeat, chives, mirin, star anise, sambal, and salt. Set aside.

Remove a few banana leaves from the package and unfold. Gently wash the leaves under cool running water and pat dry. Use a scissors to cut off the tough rib that runs along the bottom of the leaf and reserve for tying the packages later. Then cut or tear the leaves into sections roughly 8 inches square. Continue until you have 8 squares. The sections don't need to be perfect or uniform, as long as they don't have significant tears or gaps. (You won't need all the banana leaves in the package.)

Lay out the banana leaf sections and put about ¼ cup of the scallop-crab mixture in the center of each square. To form a packet, fold two sides of the banana leaf over the crab mixture, then fold in the opposite sides. Cut a length of the banana leaf rib and use it like twine to tie up the packet. Repeat until all the packets are folded and tied.

Fill a large saucepan or wok about halfway with water and bring to a boil over high heat. Divide the packets between the two steamer baskets, cover with the lid, and place over the saucepan. Steam over boiling water until the crab mixture is cooked through, about 15 minutes, switching the steamer baskets about halfway through the cooking time.

Remove the packets from the steamer baskets and serve 2 to each guest, cutting off the "twine" and partially opening the packets. Accompany each serving with a ramekin of sweet chile sauce and a lime wedge.

# CRAB AND PORK SHAO MAI

*Makes about 24 dumplings, 6 appetizer servings*

Shao-mai (pronounced shoo-MY) or gyoza wrappers, available in Asian groceries, are thin 3-inch diameter rounds. I use the Rose brand. If you buy thin square wrappers, stack them in groups of ten or so and round the corners with a pair of kitchen shears.

For steaming the shao mai, a multitiered Chinese bamboo steamer with two steaming baskets works best. Set the bamboo steamer over a wok or a large saucepan partially filled with boiling water. If you don't have a multitiered bamboo steamer, divide the dumplings between two pots with steamer baskets. (If you use metal steamer baskets instead of bamboo, lightly oil them first so the shao mai don't stick.)

You can make these ahead, chill, and reheat in the steamer baskets for about 5 minutes.

1 large egg white

1 tablespoon sake

2 teaspoons soy sauce

2 teaspoons sesame oil

2 tablespoons cornstarch, plus a little more for dusting the plate

1/2 teaspoon sugar

1 teaspoon kosher salt

1/4 teaspoon freshly ground black pepper

1 tablespoon minced scallions, white and green parts

2 teaspoons peeled and grated fresh ginger

2 teaspoons finely chopped fresh cilantro

1/4 cup drained, canned water chestnuts, coarsely chopped

1/4 cup peeled and grated carrot

1/2 pound ground pork

1/2 pound crabmeat, drained, picked clean of shell, and lightly squeezed if wet (see page 5)

1 package shao mai or gyoza wrappers

About 24 raw green peas, fresh or frozen

Cornstarch, for dusting

Chili oil or Chinese hot chili paste

In a bowl, lightly whisk together the egg white, sake, soy sauce, sesame oil, cornstarch, sugar, salt, and pepper. Add the scallions, ginger, cilantro, water chestnuts, and carrot, and stir. Add the pork and crabmeat, and mix with a rubber spatula until well combined.

Set a shao mai wrapper on a work surface and place a heaping tablespoon of filling in the center. Then gather up the edges of the wrapper, pleating it around the filling. Hold the dumpling between your thumb and index finger, squeezing it to form a "waist," while flattening the bottom of the dumpling with your other hand. The dumpling will be open on top, leaving the top of the filling exposed. Press one pea into the center of the exposed filling. Set the dumpling on a large plate lightly dusted with cornstarch. Repeat until all the crab-pork mixture is used. You should have about 24 dumplings.

Fill a large saucepan or wok about halfway with water and bring to a boil over high heat. Divide the shao mai between two bamboo steamer baskets. Stack the baskets, cover with the lid, and place over the saucepan. Steam until the shao mai are cooked through, about 15 minutes, reversing the baskets about halfway through the steaming time.

Remove the shao mai from the baskets, transfer to plates, and serve with ramekins of chili oil or chili paste.

# MASCARPONE CRAB CAKES

*Makes 8 large crab cakes*

These crab cakes are like tender, lemony, delicately flavored gnocchi dumplings, perfect for an elegant first course. In the spring, cook some warm sliced blanched asparagus, blanched peas, and the reserved crabmeat in a little butter and top the gnocchi with this mixture instead of the Tomato Relish.

Mascarpone is a buttery, rich Italian cream cheese available in cheese stores and many supermarkets.

| | | |
|---|---|---|
| ½ pound crabmeat, drained, picked clean of shell, and lightly squeezed if wet (see page 5) | 1 tablespoon plus 1½ teaspoons grated lemon zest | ¾ cup all-purpose flour |
| 1 cup mascarpone | 1 tablespoon plus 1½ teaspoons finely chopped fresh tarragon | About 2 tablespoons olive oil, for frying |
| 1 large egg yolk | ¾ teaspoon kosher salt | Fresh Tomato Relish (page 131) |
| | ½ teaspoon freshly ground black pepper | |

Preheat the oven to 400°F. Measure out about ⅓ cup of the crabmeat, especially any nice chunks of claw or leg meat, and set aside for garnish, refrigerated.

Put the mascarpone in a large bowl and mix in the egg yolk, lemon zest, tarragon, salt, and pepper until everything is well combined. Fold in the crabmeat (except for the crabmeat reserved for garnish), using a rubber spatula. Sprinkle the flour over the top, then work it in with the spatula until you have a smooth dough.

Turn the dough out onto a work surface and shape it into a log about 8 inches by 1¾ inches. Using a knife lightly dipped in flour, cut the log into 8 equal slices. Lay each slice cut

side down and flatten slightly (to about ⅔ inch thick), then set aside on a large plate.

Heat 2 large nonstick ovenproof skillets over medium heat. Add about 1 tablespoon olive oil to each pan. When the oil is hot, place 4 cakes in each pan. Fry until the cakes are golden brown on one side, about 4 minutes, turn with a spatula, and fry about 1½ minutes on the other side. Then place both pans in the oven until the cakes are cooked through, about 5 minutes.

Remove the pans from the oven, drain the cakes on paper towels if needed, and transfer to plates, serving 2 to each person. Spoon some Tomato Relish next to the crab cakes on each plate, top each serving with the reserved crab, dividing it equally, and serve.

# CRAB PAKORAS

*Makes 24, 6 servings*

These pakoras make a great appetizer, or use them as a filler for pita. Chickpea or garbanzo bean flour can be found in some supermarkets or Indian grocery stores. See "How to Deep-Fry," page 27.

1 ½ cups chickpea flour, such as Bob's Red Mill garbanzo bean flour

1 tablespoon fresh lemon juice

2 teaspoons peanut or canola oil, plus more as needed for frying

2 teaspoons Madras curry powder

2 teaspoons kosher salt

½ teaspoon turmeric

¼ teaspoon cayenne

½ cup water

1 pound crabmeat, drained, picked clean of shell, and lightly squeezed if wet (see page 5)

2 cups lightly packed spinach leaves, coarsely chopped

1 cup peeled and grated sweet potato (about ½ large sweet potato)

½ cup thinly sliced onion

2 tablespoons stemmed, seeded, and finely chopped red or green jalapeño peppers

Cucumber Yogurt (page 133)

6 lime wedges

Hot mango chutney or spicy lime pickle

In a large bowl, combine the chickpea flour, lemon juice, 2 teaspoons oil, curry powder, salt, turmeric, and cayenne. Add the water and mix well, using a rubber spatula. The batter will be very thick. Cover and allow to rest about 30 minutes.

After the batter has rested, add the crabmeat, spinach, sweet potato, onion, and jalapeños, and fold into the batter using a rubber spatula. Because the batter is thick, and because there is a large number of ingredients, it may be easier to work them in with your hands. At first it will seem that there is too little batter, but just keep mixing until you have a fairly homogenous mass.

Divide the crab mixture into 24 small mounds and form each one into a patty about 2 inches wide and ½ inch thick. Set the patties aside on a tray.

Preheat the oven to 200°F.

Clip a deep-frying thermometer to a straight-sided pan filled with 2 inches of oil. Heat the oil to 350°F, using the thermometer to maintain the temperature. Add as many patties to the oil as will fit comfortably and fry until golden brown and cooked through, turning occasionally with a slotted spoon, about 4 minutes. Remove from the oil with the slotted spoon, drain on paper towels, and keep warm in the oven while you fry the remaining pakoras.

Divide the pakoras among 6 plates. Put a big spoonful of Cucumber Yogurt and a lime wedge on each plate. Pass more of the yogurt and hot mango chutney or spicy lime pickle at the table.

★

# CRAB AND SHRIMP CAKES WITH SPICY CHIPOTLE MAYONNAISE

*Makes 8 large crab cakes*

These crab cakes came from Nancy Silverton's *Twist of the Wrist: Nancy Silverton Creates Flavorful Meals Using Ingredients from Jars, Cans, Bags, and Boxes.* Nancy's premise is that the home cook who can save time using quality packaged ingredients will cook at home more often rather than opting for takeout.

Devonshire cream is a thick English double cream, sold in refrigerated jars in gourmet supermarkets.

½ pound crabmeat, drained, picked clean of shell, and lightly squeezed if wet (see page 5)

½ pound cooked bay (baby) shrimp

One 5.6-ounce jar Devonshire cream (1 cup plus 2 tablespoons), at room temperature

12 saltine crackers, finely ground in a food processor or blender (about 6 tablespoons)

3 tablespoons finely chopped fresh chives

1 tablespoon plus 1 teaspoon fresh lemon juice

Heaping ½ teaspoon finely chopped jarred hot peppers (such as cherry peppers), stems and seeds removed

Heaping ½ teaspoon cayenne

About ½ cup all-purpose flour, for dredging

½ cup canola or peanut oil

8 cups loosely packed prewashed mixed baby greens

Spicy Chipotle Mayonnaise (page 139)

Combine the crabmeat, shrimp, Devonshire cream, saltine crumbs, chives, lemon juice, hot peppers, and cayenne together in a large bowl, and mix thoroughly. Cover and refrigerate 20 minutes.

Remove the crab and shrimp mixture from the refrigerator and form the mixture into 8 equal-size patties, about 3 inches round and ½ to ¾ inch thick. Press the cakes together firmly so they don't break apart during cooking. Pour about ½ cup flour on a plate and dredge the cakes in the flour to coat all sides.

To cook the cakes, place 2 large nonstick skillets over high heat, add ¼ cup oil to each skillet, and heat for 2 minutes. Place 4 cakes in each skillet and cook until golden brown on one side, about 1½ minutes. Turn carefully so the cakes don't break, reduce the heat to medium, and cook 1 minute on the second side. Remove the cakes from the oil and place on paper towels to drain.

Scatter the greens on each of 4 plates, dividing them evenly. Place 2 crab cakes on each plate and spoon a dollop of the Spicy Chipotle mayonnaise alongside. Serve with additional mayonnaise on the side.

★

# WILD GINGER CRAB CAKES

Rick and Ann Yoder's Wild Ginger was a groundbreaking restaurant in Seattle when it opened eighteen years ago. It remains one of my favorites. When the restaurant's cooks make these crab cakes, they steam whole live Dungeness crabs and pick out the meat themselves.

The roots of cilantro plants are often used in Asian cooking, although they're not easy to find unless you go to an Asian grocery store or a farmers' market. If you can't find cilantro roots, use the stems instead, saving the leaves for another use.

2 large eggs

1 tablespoon Southeast Asian red curry paste (such as Mae Ploy brand)

2 green onions, minced, white parts only

2 tablespoons minced shallots

1 tablespoon plus 1½ teaspoons minced cilantro root or stems

1½ teaspoons peeled and grated fresh ginger

1 pound fresh crabmeat, drained, picked clean of shell, and lightly squeezed if wet (see page 5)

2 cups panko (see page 10)

Peanut or canola oil, as needed for frying

Lime Dipping Sauce (page 141)

In a large bowl with a whisk lightly beat the eggs. Add the curry paste and whisk until combined. Using a rubber spatula, mix in the green onions, shallots, cilantro stems, and ginger. When everything is well combined, stir in the crabmeat.

Spread 1½ cups of the panko in a shallow container. Divide the crab mixture into 8 mounds and form them into patties, dropping them in the container of crumbs. Sprinkle on as much of the remaining panko as needed to cover the tops of the patties. Cover the crab cakes with plastic wrap and refrigerate for about 30 minutes. (These crab cakes don't sit well overnight.)

When you are ready to fry the crab cakes, place 2 large nonstick or cast-iron skillets over medium-high heat and pour in enough oil to coat the bottoms of the pans about ⅛ inch deep. When the oil is hot, shake excess panko from the patties, add 4 patties to each pan, and reduce the heat to medium. Fry until the crab cakes are golden brown and heated through, turning once with a spatula to brown both sides, 3 to 4 minutes per side, turning the heat down as needed so they don't brown too quickly. The internal temperature of a crab cake should read 155°F on an instant-read thermometer. Remove the crab cakes from the pan and drain on paper towels.

Transfer the crab cakes to plates, serving each person 2 crab cakes and a ramekin of Lime Dipping Sauce.

# CRAB CAKE STUFFED MUSHROOMS

*Makes 12 stuffed mushrooms, 4 appetizer servings*

A crab-stuffed mushroom is a no-brainer when it comes to dreaming up a popular appetizer. A smaller amount of **Steven's Perfect Dungeness Crab Cakes (page 20)** is stuffed into large button mushroom caps, then topped with buttery herbed bread crumbs. Serve these crabby morsels with glasses of champagne. The recipe can be easily doubled or tripled, so keep these in mind for **Christmas Eve or New Year's Eve**.

¼ pound crabmeat, drained, picked clean of shell, and lightly squeezed if wet (see page 5)

2 tablespoons plus 1½ teaspoons mayonnaise

2 teaspoons grated lemon zest

2 teaspoons minced fresh dill

1 tablespoon thinly sliced chives

2 tablespoons panko (see page 10)

Kosher salt and freshly ground black pepper

1½ teaspoons unsalted butter

3 tablespoons dried bread crumbs (see page 7)

2 teaspoons chopped parsley

2 tablespoons grated Parmesan

12 large button mushrooms, 1½ to 2 inches wide (about ¾ pound)

1 tablespoon plus 1½ teaspoons olive oil

To make the crab cake stuffing, put the crabmeat, mayonnaise, lemon zest, dill, and 2 teaspoons of the chives in a bowl. Mix everything together gently with a rubber spatula. Add the panko and mix again. Season to taste with salt and pepper. Cover and set aside, refrigerated. To make the toasted bread crumbs, melt the butter in a small skillet over medium heat.

Add the crumbs and stir a few minutes until browned and crunchy. Remove from the heat and stir in the parsley, remaining 1 teaspoon chives, and the Parmesan. Season to taste with salt and pepper. Set aside.

Preheat the broiler.

Gently remove the stem from each mushroom by wiggling it from side to side until you can pop it out. If any stem remains, use a small spoon to scrape it out, being careful not to break the cap. Discard the stems or save them for another use. Put the mushrooms in a bowl and toss them with the olive oil. Season the mushrooms to taste with salt and pepper. Spread the mushrooms on a baking sheet, stemmed side up, and place under the broiler until they are cooked, about 4 minutes.

Remove the mushrooms from the broiler and preheat the oven to 400°F. Drain the mushrooms upside down on a paper towel–lined plate, to remove any liquid that has collected while they were cooking. Return the caps to the baking sheet, stemmed sides up. Divide the crab cake mixture among the mushrooms, firmly mounding it over each cap. Sprinkle the toasted bread crumbs evenly over the stuffing. Place the baking sheet in the oven and bake until the mushrooms are heated through, about 10 minutes. Remove the baking sheet from the oven, transfer the mushrooms to a platter, let cool for a minute or two, and then serve.

★

# ARTICHOKE STUFFED SOFT-SHELL CRAB "CAKES"

*Makes 4 servings*

Blue crabs don't have a growth gene in their shells, so they have to shed the shells when they grow. It's at this point that the treasured soft-shell crab comes to market.

Cut into one of these gorgeously golden brown potato chip–crusted crabs to get to the creamy artichoke filling tucked inside. This is one rich dish, so plan on one large soft-shell per person.

2 cooked artichoke bottoms (see page 83), cut into small dice (about ½ cup)

¼ cup drained, canned water chestnuts, coarsely chopped

2 tablespoons mayonnaise

2 tablespoons sour cream

¼ cup grated Parmesan

½ teaspoon kosher salt

¼ teaspoon freshly ground black pepper

4 "prime" soft-shell crabs (4½ to 5 inches), live or thawed

8 cups potato chips (about 6 ounces)

1½ cups panko (see page 10)

1 cup all-purpose flour

2 large eggs, lightly beaten with ¼ cup water

Peanut or canola oil, for frying

1 small bunch watercress sprigs, tough stems discarded

4 lemon wedges

Preheat the oven to 400°F.

Put the artichokes, water chestnuts, mayonnaise, sour cream, Parmesan, salt, and pepper in a bowl, and stir to combine. Set aside, covered and refrigerated.

To clean a soft-shell crab (frozen soft-shell crabs may or may not already have been cleaned), set it on a work surface, shell side up. Using a pair of sharp scissors, cut off the eyes and mouth, making a straight cut across the face. Lift up the points (the pointed ends of the

shell) on opposite sides of the crab and pull out or cut off the spongy gills underneath. In the same area, you'll find a yellow sand sac (stomach) and what some people call the "mustard." It's up to you whether to remove this or not. Some people love it and some find it bitter. Then turn the crab over and pull out the apron (abdomen) and cut it off. Repeat with the remaining crabs.

On the side of the crab where the face was cut off, there's a pocket between the shell and the crabmeat. Pick up one of the crabs and spoon about one-quarter of the filling into the pocket, or as much as will fit. Repeat with the remaining crabs.

In a food processor, process the potato chips until they are finely crushed. Add the panko and pulse a few times. Set out 3 shallow containers. Put the flour in one container, the egg wash in the second container, and the potato-chip mixture in the third. Put a crab in the flour and dredge it on both sides, shaking off excess flour. Then drop the crab into the egg wash, turning it to coat all sides. Pick up the crab and drop it into the potato-chip mixture, turning it several times to coat all sides well, then remove the breaded crab to a large plate. Repeat with the remaining crabs.

Put 2 large nonstick or cast-iron skillets over high heat and pour in enough oil to coat the bottoms of the pans about ¼ inch deep. When the oil is hot, put 2 crabs in each pan. Fry until crusty and golden brown on the first side, 2 to 3 minutes, turning the heat down to medium after about a minute, then turn the crabs to brown the other side, about 2 minutes more.

Transfer the crabs to a baking sheet and place them in the oven. Bake until the crabs are cooked and hot through, 6 to 8 minutes. Remove from the oven and drain the crabs on paper towels.

Transfer the crabs to plates and garnish each plate with a little bunch of watercress and a lemon wedge. Serve immediately.

★

# Cooked Artichoke Bottoms

Using a serrated knife, slice off the top 1½ inches of the artichokes and place in a large saucepan with enough cold water to cover. Squeeze half a lemon into the pan, add a cup of dry white wine and a few chunks of onion and carrot. To keep the artichokes submerged while they cook, put a sheet of parchment or wax paper on the surface and weight it with a plate or a small lid. Bring the liquid to a boil, then reduce the heat to a simmer and continue to cook until the artichoke is completely tender, 30 to 45 minutes, depending on size. Test an artichoke; it should be easily pierced with the tip of a knife. Remove the artichokes from the pot. When the artichokes are cool enough to handle, pull off and discard all of the leaves. Scoop out the choke with a teaspoon and discard. With a sharp knife, trim away any tough parts of the stem and around the artichoke bottom.

# FRITO PIE CRAB CAKES

*Makes 4 large crab cakes*

Chef Adam Perry Lang of Daisy May's BBQ in Manhattan has a knack for making food from and for the soul. These golden Frito-crusted cakes are Adam's version of Frito Pie, a retro dish of hot chili ladled over Frito corn chips, popular in New Mexico and Texas.

Adam prefers Chimayo chili powder, which is made from New Mexican chiles and is available in Latino grocery stores, but you could substitute any mild chili powder.

Adam serves his crab cakes with a dark, reddish brown Chimayo chile sauce and crispy fried pork rinds, but they're great with just about any kind of salsa.

1 large egg

2 tablespoons chopped fresh cilantro

1 tablespoon fresh lemon juice

1½ teaspoons mayonnaise

1½ teaspoons milk

¾ teaspoon Worcestershire sauce

½ teaspoon Chimayo chili powder, or other chili powder

¼ teaspoon kosher salt

1¼ cups fresh bread crumbs (see page 7)

1 pound lump blue crabmeat, drained and picked clean of shell

3 cups corn chips, preferably Fritos

1½ cups panko (see page 10)

1 cup masa harina (see page 9)

2 large eggs, lightly beaten with 2 tablespoons water

2 tablespoons peanut or canola oil

2 tablespoons unsalted butter

Sour cream

Roasted Tomatillo Salsa (page 136)

To make the crab cakes, put the egg, cilantro, lemon juice, mayonnaise, milk, Worcestershire sauce, chili powder, and salt in a large bowl, and whisk to combine. Stir in the bread crumbs with a rubber spatula, then mix in the crabmeat, combining everything well. Divide the mixture into 4 mounds and shape into 4 patties. Put the patties on a large plate, cover with plastic wrap, and chill for an hour or longer.

To bread the crab cakes, process the corn chips in a food processor until they are finely crushed. Add the panko and process a few times. Set out 3 shallow containers. Put the masa harina in the first container, the egg wash in the second container, and the corn-chip mixture in the third container. Put one of the patties into the first container, dredging or sprinkling it on both sides with the masa harina, then transfer it to the container of egg wash. Turn to coat both sides, then place the crab cake in the panko. Dredge or sprinkle the patty to coat evenly and thoroughly with crumbs on both sides. Then gently shake off excess crumbs and place the patty on a large plate. (If the patties seem fragile, it may be easier to use a spatula to transfer the patties from pan to pan rather than using your hands.) Repeat for the remaining patties.

To fry the crab cakes, preheat the oven to 350°F. Put 2 large nonstick ovenproof skillets over medium-high heat and put 1 tablespoon oil and 1 tablespoon butter in each pan. When the butter has melted, put 2 patties in each pan. Cook until the patties are golden brown on the first side, about 3 minutes, then flip and cook 2 more minutes on the second side. Place the skillets in the oven and bake until the crab cakes are heated through, about 8 minutes. Remove from the oven.

Transfer the crab cakes to 4 plates, and serve with a spoonful of sour cream and a dollop of Roasted Tomatillo Salsa.

★

# ROASTED FENNEL CRAB CAKES

**Caprial and John Pence are neighbors here in the Northwest, right "next door" in Portland, Oregon, where they own Caprial's Bistro. It's always a delight to share a glass of wine with them, especially when we can have a plate of these crab cakes. A lively French rouille of sweet red peppers, pungent with anchovies and garlic, makes a good match with the roasted fennel flavor of the cakes. When you trim the fennel bulb, be sure to save some of the greens for seasoning the crab cakes.**

1 large fennel bulb, trimmed and cut into large dice (about 1¼ pounds before trimming)

4 shallots, quartered

¼ cup olive oil

Kosher salt

Freshly ground black pepper

⅔ cup milk

½ teaspoon chopped garlic

1 tablespoon unsalted butter, softened

1 tablespoon plus 1½ teaspoons all-purpose flour, plus 1 cup more for dredging

1 pound crabmeat, drained, picked clean of shell, and lightly squeezed if wet (see page 5)

1 large egg, lightly beaten

1 tablespoon chopped fresh fennel greens

1 tablespoon grated lemon zest

2 teaspoons chopped fresh thyme

4 tablespoons olive oil

Red Pepper Rouille (page 143)

To roast the vegetables for the crab cakes, preheat the oven to 375°F. Place the fennel and shallots in a roasting pan and drizzle with the olive oil. Season to taste with salt and pepper, then roast the vegetables until tender and lightly browned, 40 to 45 minutes, stirring a few times. Allow to cool.

To make the béchamel, combine the milk and garlic in a saucepan over medium-high heat and heat the mixture until just under a boil. Meanwhile, in a small bowl, mix together the butter and the 1 tablespoon plus 1½ teaspoons flour until a soft dough forms. Whisk the butter-flour mixture into the milk. Cook, whisking often, until the sauce bubbles and thickens, 3 to 4 minutes. Season to taste with salt and pepper. Strain the sauce through a fine sieve and allow to cool.

To assemble the crab cakes, coarsely chop the fennel and shallots and place in a bowl. Add the crabmeat, egg, béchamel, fennel greens, lemon zest, and thyme, and mix well. Season to taste with salt and pepper (about 1 teaspoon salt and ½ teaspoon pepper). Form the mixture into 8 patties, about 2½ inches wide and ¾ inch thick. If time permits, cover with plastic wrap and chill 30 minutes or more.

To fry the crab cakes, spread the 1 cup flour on a plate and dredge the patties lightly on both sides. Heat 2 large nonstick skillets over medium-high heat and add 2 tablespoons of oil to each pan. When the pans are hot, place 4 patties in each pan. Turn the heat down to medium and fry the crab cakes until golden and heated through, turning once with a spatula to brown both sides, about 4 minutes per side.

Transfer the crab cakes to 4 plates, serving 2 to each person, with a spoonful of Red Pepper Rouille on the side.

★

# BRUNCH AND BREAKFAST CRAB CAKES

# SMOKED SALMON CRAB CAKES

*Makes 4 large crab cakes*

Set one of these next to a couple of fried eggs with a slab of toasted and buttered baguette, and call it Sunday brunch. I prefer a good-quality hard-smoked salmon, but lox will work fine if you can get the less salty Nova style.

1 large egg

2 tablespoons sour cream

$1/4$ pound crabmeat, drained, picked clean of shell, and lightly squeezed if wet (see page 5)

$1/4$ pound smoked salmon, finely chopped

1 tablespoon plus 2 teaspoons minced parsley

2 teaspoons grated lemon zest

$1/4$ teaspoon freshly ground black pepper

$1/8$ teaspoon cayenne

$1/2$ cup fresh bread crumbs (see page 7)

$1/2$ cup dried bread crumbs (see page 7), for dredging

About 2 tablespoons unsalted butter

Lemon Dill Cream (page 130)

In a medium bowl, whisk together the egg and sour cream. Using a rubber spatula, mix in the crabmeat, salmon, parsley, lemon zest, pepper, and cayenne until well combined. Then fold in the fresh bread crumbs. Divide the mixture into 4 mounds and form into 4 patties. Place the patties on a large plate, cover with plastic wrap, and refrigerate at least 30 minutes.

When ready to fry the crab cakes, spread the dried bread crumbs on a large plate. Lightly sprinkle the cakes with bread crumbs on both sides. Place a large nonstick skillet over medium heat and add about 2 tablespoons butter to the pan. When the butter is melted, place all the patties in the pan and fry until golden brown on both sides and hot through, turning once with a spatula, about 4 minutes per side. The internal temperature of a crab cake should read 155°F on an instant-read thermometer.

Transfer the crab cakes to 4 plates, serving 1 per person, and serve with the Lemon Dill Cream as an appetizer or as part of a brunch menu.

# MR. JOE'S TOMATO GRAVY CRAB CAKES WITH SMOKY BACON

*Makes 8 servings*

Mr. Joe was our next-door neighbor when I was growing up in Newark, Delaware. On weekends, he'd sometimes have my family over and serve us toast smothered with gravy made from bacon grease and canned tomato sauce. I love Mr. Joe's tomato gravy so much, this is the second book I'm putting his recipe in, but I've added crab cakes. These make a spectacular brunch for your friends and family.

Instead of the Chesapeake Bay Classic Crab Cakes, you can use Emeril's Crab Cakes (page 22) or Jazz Fest Crab and Crayfish Cakes (page 28).

Mr. Joe used plenty of Tabasco in his gravy, but you can suit the amount to your taste.

16 slices thick-cut bacon, about a pound

⅔ cup chopped onion

1½ cups canned diced or crushed tomatoes

1 cup canned tomato sauce

1 to 2 teaspoons Tabasco, or more to taste

2 teaspoons sugar

Kosher salt and freshly ground black pepper

1 teaspoon cornstarch, dissolved in 1 tablespoon cold water

1 recipe Chesapeake Bay Classic Crab Cakes (page 15), shaped into 8 cakes, uncooked

About 4 tablespoons unsalted butter, plus more for buttering the toast

16 slices baguette, cut on an angle ½ inch thick, or 8 slices rustic bread

2 tablespoons chopped parsley

To make the tomato gravy, fry the bacon in a large skillet until crispy. (If you don't have a 12-inch skillet use 2 skillets to fry the bacon.) Set the bacon aside to garnish the crab cakes later. Leave 2 tablespoons of the bacon fat in the skillet and discard the rest or save for another use. In the same pan over medium heat, cook the onion in the bacon fat, stirring as needed, 2 to 3 minutes. Add the diced or crushed tomatoes and the tomato sauce and simmer for 10 minutes. Remove the tomato gravy from the pan and coarsely puree in a food processor or a blender. Return the gravy to the skillet and season with Tabasco, sugar, salt, and pepper to taste. Add the dissolved cornstarch to the sauce and simmer another 5 minutes, stirring often. Keep the sauce warm, and preheat the broiler.

To fry the crab cakes, put 2 large nonstick skillets over medium heat. Add about 2 tablespoons butter to each pan. When the butter is melted, add 4 crab cakes to each pan, shaking off the excess crumbs first. Slowly fry the crab cakes until they are golden brown on both sides and hot through, turning once with a spatula, about 4 minutes a side. If the crab cakes are browning too quickly, reduce the heat. The internal temperature of a crab cake should be 155°F on an instant-read thermometer.

Meanwhile, place the baguette or rustic bread slices on a baking sheet and toast under the broiler, turning them once, until the bread is a light golden brown on both sides. Remove the bread and spread each slice lightly with butter. Put the reserved bacon strips in a pan and reheat them briefly under the broiler.

Set out 8 plates and put 2 slices of baguette or 1 slice of rustic bread on each plate. Set a crab cake on top of one of the slices on each plate. Ladle some of the tomato gravy onto each plate, draping it partially over the toast and crab cake. Top each serving with 2 slices of bacon, sprinkle with some of the parsley, and serve.

# CRAB POTATO PANCAKES

*Makes 10, 4 to 5 servings*

**Adding a little crabmeat to a batch of crusty, golden potato pancakes makes for a glorious brunch.**

1½ pounds large Yukon gold or russet potatoes, peeled

1 small onion, peeled (about 6 ounces)

¾ pound crabmeat, drained, picked clean of shell, and lightly squeezed if wet (see page 5)

3 large eggs, lightly beaten

4 tablespoons and 2 teaspoons dried bread crumbs (see page 7)

1½ teaspoons kosher salt

¾ teaspoon freshly ground black pepper

Peanut or canola oil, for frying

Lemon Dill Cream (page 130)

Preheat the oven to 200°F.

Grate the potatoes and the onion, using a box grater or the medium grating blade of a food processor. Lay a large piece of cheesecloth or a clean dishcloth in a large bowl, and pour in the potato-onion mixture. Gather up the edges of the cloth, forcing the grated vegetables into a tight bundle, and wring out as much liquid as you can, discarding the liquid.

Shake the potato-onion mixture into a large bowl. Stir in the crabmeat, eggs, bread

Clip a deep-fry thermometer to a straight-sided pot. Fill the pot with at least 2 inches oil and heat to 350°F, maintaining the temperature with the thermometer. Drop as many of the balls into the oil as will fit comfortably, and fry until golden and cooked through, about 4 minutes total time, turning occasionally with a slotted spoon. Remove from the oil, drain on paper towels, and keep warm while you continue frying the rest of the balls.

Transfer the hush crabbies to plates and serve with the Spicy Remoulade or Spicy Corn Tartar Sauce.

# CRAB CAKES HUEVOS

*Makes 8 servings*

Costco Quickie crab cakes, spiked with chili powder and Cheddar cheese, are a natural served huevos-style on a fried tortilla with savory black beans. If you want to go whole hog, add a fried or poached egg to each plate.

Note that the black beans take a few hours to cook. You can cook them a day ahead and refrigerate them.

2 cups dried black beans, picked over and rinsed

1 tablespoon plus 1 teaspoon olive oil

½ cup chopped onion

1½ teaspoons minced garlic

1 tablespoon pureed canned chipotle peppers in adobo (see page 8)

Kosher salt

Freshly ground black pepper

Peanut or canola oil, for frying

8 corn or flour tortillas

1 recipe Costco Quickie crab cakes (page 24), formed into 8 cakes, uncooked

Sour cream

Roasted Tomatillo Salsa (page 136) or Tomato-Avocado Salsa (page 135)

2 tablespoons minced scallions, white and green parts

Put the beans in a pot and cover generously with water. Bring to a boil, then turn the heat down to a simmer and cook until the beans are tender, 1½ to 2 hours. Drain, reserving 1½ cups cooking liquid.

Heat the olive oil in a large saucepan over medium-high heat. Add the onion and sauté until softened, about 3 minutes. Add the garlic and sauté 1 minute more. Add the black beans, chipotle, and the reserved cooking liquid, and season to taste with salt and pepper. Simmer 5 minutes until heated through, then set aside.

Heat a large skillet over medium-high heat and pour in enough oil to coat the bottom of

the pan about ¼ inch deep. When the oil is hot, fry the tortillas on both sides until browned and crispy, about 1 minute per side or slightly less. Drain the tortillas on paper towels, transfer them to a baking sheet, and set aside.

Preheat the oven to 400°F.

To cook the crab cakes, place 2 large nonstick skillets over medium heat and add 2 tablespoons oil to each skillet. When the pans are hot, add 4 cakes to each pan. Fry until golden brown and hot through, turning once with a spatula, about 4 minutes per side.

Meanwhile, briefly heat the tortillas in the oven and bring the beans back to a simmer.

Set out 8 plates. Put a warm tortilla on each plate, spoon some of the beans into each tortilla, top with a crab cake, spoon some sour cream and Roasted Tomatillo Salsa alongside, and scatter scallions over the top. Serve immediately.

# CRAB CAKE SANDWICHES

# CHESAPEAKE BAY CLASSIC CRAB CAKE SANDWICHES

*Makes 6*

Broiled or fried, platter or sandwich, those are the toughest decisions to make when you're on vacation on the Eastern Shore. A plump, juicy sandwich with fried crab cakes, a side of fries, and some sweet and sour coleslaw and you've got heaven on a bun.

About 4 tablespoons unsalted butter, plus a little more for buttering the buns

1 recipe Chesapeake Bay Classic Crab Cakes (page 15), shaped into 6 patties instead of 8, uncooked

6 hamburger buns or Kaiser rolls, split

6 slices tomato

3 cups shredded iceberg lettuce

Preheat the broiler.

Put 2 large nonstick skillets over medium-high heat and add about 2 tablespoons butter to each pan. When the butter is melted, add 3 patties to each pan. Slowly fry the crab cakes over medium heat until they are golden brown on both sides and hot through, turning once with a spatula, about 4 minutes per side. The internal temperature of a crab cake should read 155°F on an instant-read thermometer. If the crab cakes are browning too quickly, reduce the heat.

Meanwhile, toast the split buns under the broiler until they are light golden. Remove the buns and spread both split sides of each bun lightly with butter.

When the crab cakes are cooked, place 1 crab cake on the bottom half of a bun. Top with a tomato slice and some of the lettuce. Put the other half of the bun on top. Repeat for the other sandwiches, transfer to plates, and serve immediately.

# BCCLT SANDWICHES

*Makes 6*

**BCCLT** means bacon, crab cake, lettuce, and tomato, of course. And, as we all know, bacon makes everything better. When shaping crab cakes for sandwiches, I flatten them a bit more than usual so they don't squeeze out the sides of the bread or bun when you're eating one, and the crust area is crunchier.

| | | |
|---|---|---|
| 18 slices thick-cut bacon (a little more than a pound) | 1 recipe Chesapeake Bay Classic Crab Cakes (page 15), shaped into 6 flattened patties, about ½ inch thick, instead of 8, uncooked | 12 slices firm-textured white sandwich bread, such as Pepperidge Farm |
| About 4 tablespoons unsalted butter, plus more for buttering the toast | | 6 slices tomato |
| | | 6 butter lettuce leaves |

Preheat the oven to 400°F. Put the bacon on a baking sheet, place it in the oven, and cook until crisp, 8 to 10 minutes. Remove the bacon from the pan, drain on paper towels, and set aside.

Preheat the broiler.

Put 2 large nonstick skillets over medium heat and add about 2 tablespoons butter to each pan. Add 3 patties to each pan and slowly fry them until they are golden brown on both sides and hot through, turning once with a spatula, 4 to 5 minutes per side. The internal temperature of a crab cake should read 155°F on an instant-read thermometer.

Meanwhile, place the bread on a baking sheet and toast under the broiler, turning, until the bread is a light golden brown on both sides. Remove the bread and spread each slice lightly with butter. Put the reserved cooked bacon on a baking sheet and warm it briefly under the broiler.

When the crab cakes are cooked, place 1 crab cake on a piece of toast, buttered side up. Top with 3 pieces of bacon. Top with a tomato slice and lettuce leaves. Place a second slice of toast on top, buttered side down. Repeat for the other sandwiches, transfer to plates, and serve immediately.

# BABE'S VERDE CRAB CAKE BURGERS

*Makes 6*

My friend Babe Shepherd owns, with her brother, two wildly popular burger joints in Seattle called Red Mill Burgers. One of her top-selling items is the fabulous Verde Burger, topped with melted Jack cheese and a roasted green chile. Babe's crew hand-peels forty pounds of chiles a day to keep up with demand. Here's my tribute to Babe.

4 tablespoons unsalted butter

1 recipe Etta's New Dungeness Crab Cakes (page 18), shaped into 6 patties instead of 8, uncooked

6 hamburger buns, split

Spicy Chipotle Mayonnaise (page 139)

6 slices Jack cheese, about 1 ounce each

3 large poblano peppers, roasted, peeled, split open, and seeded (see page 62)

Preheat the broiler and place 2 large nonstick skillets over medium heat. Add 2 tablespoons butter to each pan. When the butter has melted, add 3 patties to each pan. Gently fry the crab cakes until they are golden brown on both sides and hot through, carefully turning once with a spatula, about 4 minutes per side. The internal temperature of a crab cake should read 155°F on an instant-read thermometer. If the crab cakes are browning too quickly, reduce the heat.

Meanwhile, place the split burger buns on a baking sheet, cut sides up, and toast them under the broiler until they are a light golden brown. Remove them from the oven and lightly spread both sides of each bun with some of the chipotle mayonnaise. Take the top halves of the buns off the baking sheet and set aside. Place 1 crab cake on each of the bottom halves of the buns. Top each crab cake with a slice of cheese. Place the baking sheet under the broiler until the cheese melts. Remove the baking sheet from the oven and top each cheese-covered crab cake with half a poblano pepper. Place the reserved top halves of the buns on top, transfer to plates, and serve.

# CRAB CAKE PO'BOY WITH MUFFULETTA OLIVE SALAD

*Makes 6*

The first muffuletta sandwich I ever encountered was at New Orleans' Central Grocery. I love the pickle-y, olive-y, juicy salad that they slather on top of the sliced meats and cheeses. Giardiniera is an Italian-style mixed pickle sold in glass jars, which typically contains pearl onions, cauliflower, red peppers, cucumbers, carrots, and celery.

Don't use a bread that's too dense or heavy or one with too hard a crust, or the sandwich will be difficult to eat.

1 jar (16 ounces) Italian giardiniera, such as Mezzetta brand

½ cup coarsely chopped pimento-stuffed green olives

½ cup extra virgin olive oil

3 tablespoons chopped parsley

¼ teaspoon freshly ground black pepper

1 recipe Jazz Fest Crab and Crayfish Cakes (page 28), shaped into 12 small patties instead of 8, uncooked

Spicy Remoulade (page 134)

6 pieces French bread, cut into 6-inch lengths and split lengthwise

To make the muffuletta olive salad, put the contents of the jar of giardiniera in a sieve, drain off the liquid, then transfer the vegetables to a cutting board. Stem and seed any whole peppers, then coarsely chop all the vegetables. (You should have about 2 cups.) Put the vegetables in a bowl with the olives, ¼ cup of the olive oil, the parsley, and pepper, and mix well. Set aside.

Place 2 large nonstick skillets over medium heat and pour 2 tablespoons olive oil into each pan. Add 6 patties to each pan and fry until golden brown on both sides and hot through, turning once with a spatula, 3 to 4 minutes per side. The internal temperature of a crab cake should read 155°F on an instant-read thermometer.

Meanwhile, pull out a bit of the insides from both cut sides of a 6-inch length of bread. Spread the bottom half of the bread with some remoulade, then place 2 crab cakes over it. Scoop some muffuletta salad onto the top half, being sure to drizzle on some of the juices. Gently press the 2 sides of the sandwich together. Repeat for the remaining sandwiches, cut the sandwiches in half, transfer to plates, and serve.

# PAKORA POCKET SANDWICHES

*Makes 6*

Naan, a flat Indian bread, would be ideal here, but pita also works well.

| Six 6-inch pita breads (with pockets) | 1 recipe Crab Pakoras (page 72), fried | Cucumber Yogurt (page 133) 12 tomato slices, cut in half |

Preheat the oven to 350°F. Cut the pitas in half, arrange in 2 stacks, wrap each stack in foil, and heat in the oven for 10 minutes. If the pakoras need to be warmed, put them on a baking sheet and warm for 5 minutes in the oven also.

Remove the pitas and pakoras from the oven. Fill each pita half pocket with 2 pakoras, a big spoonful of Cucumber Yogurt, and a few tomato slices.

Transfer to plates, serving 2 half pockets to each person.

# COOL CRAB CAKES

oven and pour in enough hot water to come about halfway up the sides of the muffin pan. Bake for 35 minutes. The tops of the cheesecakes will be slightly puffed and lightly browned. Remove the roasting pan from the oven and remove the muffin pan. Allow the pan to cool, then place in the refrigerator overnight, covering loosely with plastic wrap when the cheese-cakes are completely cold.

When you are ready to serve the cheesecakes, remove the muffin pan from the refrigerator and place it in a roasting pan. Fill the roasting pan with enough hot tap water to come about halfway up the sides of the muffin tin. Let the muffin pan sit in the hot water about 30 seconds (which warms the butter and makes the cakes easier to remove), then remove the pan. To unmold a cheesecake, run a small knife around the edge and, using the knife and your fingers, gently pop the cake out of the pan. Repeat until all the cheesecakes are unmolded. Place the cheesecakes on small plates.

To serve, top each cheesecake with a small dollop of Red Cocktail Sauce, then with a small mound of shredded lettuce, then with some of the crabmeat, dividing the crabmeat evenly. Top each portion of crabmeat with another dollop of cocktail sauce. Serve the cheesecakes, passing more cocktail sauce at the table.

★

# AVOCADO AND CRAB SALAD "CAKES" WITH SPICY MAYO

*Makes 4 servings*

These dramatic towers of fresh crab salad and avocado slices are easily shaped with the help of ring molds. You'll need 4 molds about 2½ inches in diameter and 3 inches deep. Deep, round, open-ended metal molds or cutters can be found in kitchenware stores. Or use 2-inch lengths of PVC pipe from the hardware store, or empty 8-ounce tomato sauce cans (tops and bottoms removed) that have been sterilized in the dishwasher. Served with crusty baguettes, these "cakes" make a stunning lunch or a substantial first course.

¾ cup mayonnaise

2 tablespoons fresh lemon juice

1½ teaspoons sriracha or sambal (see page 10)

½ teaspoon sesame oil

Kosher salt and freshly ground black pepper

6 tablespoons heavy cream

1 tablespoon whole-grain mustard

½ pound crabmeat, drained, picked clean of shell, and squeezed if wet (see page 5)

3 ripe avocados, as needed

4 teaspoons tobiko (flying-fish roe), salmon roe, or other caviar

To make the spicy mayonnaise, combine the mayonnaise, lemon juice, sriracha, and sesame oil in a small bowl. Season to taste with salt and pepper, and set aside.

To make the crab salad, whip the cream to soft mounds, using an electric mixer or a whisk. Stir in the mustard, then fold in the crabmeat, and season to taste with salt and pepper.

Slice the avocados in half, remove the pits, and remove the avocado meat from the skins, using a large spoon. Cut the avocados crosswise into ½-inch thick slices.

Set out 4 small plates and place a ring mold in the center of each plate. Attractively arrange enough avocado slices in the ring molds to completely cover the bottoms of the molds with the curved sides of the avocado facing out. At least half the avocado slices should be left over. Divide the crab salad between the 4 ring molds, smoothing the tops of the salads with the back of a spoon. Arrange as many of the remaining avocado slices as needed to cover the crab salad in the ring molds. Spoon some of the spicy mayonnaise over the tops of the molds. Put about a teaspoon of caviar on top of the mayonnaise in each mold and remove the molds by gently lifting them straight up. Serve immediately.

# TOMATO ASPIC CRAB CAKES

*Makes 4 servings*

Grandma Fogarty often made tomato aspic, which I hated as a kid. But now it brings back warm memories of her and her role as the mentor of my cooking instincts and, frankly, it tastes pretty darn good.

You will need four 6-ounce molds for this recipe. I like to use ring-shaped molds; mine are 5 inches wide and ¾ inch deep, but you can use any type of 6-ounce mold and spoon the crabmeat mixture over the tops instead of filling the center of the rings.

Vegetable oil spray or flavorless vegetable oil

2 medium ripe tomatoes (about 1 pound), stemmed, cored, and coarsely chopped

½ medium carrot (about 2 ounces), peeled and chopped

1 tablespoon seeded and chopped jalapeño pepper

1 tablespoon thinly sliced chives

2 teaspoons Tabasco

2 teaspoons prepared horse-radish

½ teaspoon kosher salt

¼ teaspoon freshly ground black pepper

½ cup dry white wine

1 tablespoon plus ¾ teaspoon unflavored gelatin (about 1½ packets)

¾ pound crabmeat, drained, picked clean of shell, and lightly squeezed if wet (see page 5)

½ cup Really Good Tartar Sauce (page 128)

½ cup loosely packed celery leaves

Set out four 6-ounce ring-shaped molds and spray or brush the interiors lightly with vegetable oil.

Put the tomatoes, carrot, jalapeño, chives, Tabasco, horseradish, salt, and pepper in a blender, and process until smooth, about 2 minutes. Pour the tomato puree into a bowl.

Put ¼ cup of the wine in a small bowl and sprinkle with the gelatin. Let the mixture stand greased cups of the mini muffin pan with the batter, dividing the batter evenly. (The cups will be about ½ full.)

Put the muffin pan in the oven and bake until the popovers are puffed and golden, about 25 minutes. Remove the pan from the oven and poke each popover with a skewer to let steam escape.

While the popovers are baking, make the crab filling. Put the crabmeat, sour cream, tarragon, lemon juice, shallot, and cayenne in a bowl, and stir gently to combine. Season to taste with salt.

Remove the popovers from the pan. Poke a hole in the top of each popover with the tip of a small knife and use your fingers to pull the edges of the hole apart, creating an opening. Spoon in the filling, dividing it evenly among the popovers. Set the popovers on a platter and sprinkle with the remaining chives. Serve immediately.

★

# CRAB POKE CAKES

Poke (po-KAY) is a popular Hawaiian dish, often made with finely diced raw ahi tuna, sesame oil, seaweed, and soy sauce, though there are many variations. This version makes an elegant appetizer, or instead of using ring molds, fry up some extra wontons and just serve the crab poke in a bowl with wonton chips on the side for a Hawaiian chip-and-dip.

You'll need 4 ring molds, about 2 or 2 1/2 inches in diameter and 2 inches deep (see page 117).

Peanut or canola oil, as needed for frying

8 wonton wrappers

1/2 pound crabmeat, drained and picked clean of shell

1/3 cup finely chopped ogo seaweed or ocean salad

1/4 cup finely diced onion

1/4 cup thinly sliced scallions, white and green parts

1 small red jalapeño pepper, stemmed, seeded, and finely minced (about 1 teaspoon)

1 tablespoon soy sauce

1 teaspoon sesame oil

1/8 teaspoon freshly ground black pepper

4 teaspoons tobiko (flying-fish roe), salmon roe, or other caviar

Clip a deep-frying thermometer to the side of a straight-sided pot. Fill with at least 2 inches oil and heat to 350°F, maintaining the temperature with the thermometer.

Stack the wonton wrappers and use a knife to cut the stack into 4 wedges. Fry the wonton chips, turning once, until golden and crisp, 30 to 40 seconds. Remove from the oil, drain on paper towels, and set aside.

Combine the crabmeat, seaweed, onion, scallions, and jalapeño in a bowl. Drizzle the soy sauce and sesame oil over the top, sprinkle with pepper, and mix with a rubber spatula until everything is well combined. Set out 4 small plates and place a ring mold in the center of each

plate. Divide the crab mixture evenly among the molds, packing the mixture into each mold with your fingers or the back of a spoon. Gently slip off the molds, pushing down on the crabmeat with your fingers as you pull up on the mold if necessary. Top each poke cake with a teaspoon of caviar, surround with some of the wonton chips, and serve.

# SAUCES
# AND
# SALSAS

# REALLY GOOD TARTAR SAUCE

*Makes about 1⅓ cups*

This is **Chris Schlesinger's** recipe for tartar sauce. He makes it with olive oil, but I prefer a flavorless oil like peanut or canola. See page 8 about egg safety.

2 large egg yolks

2 tablespoons cider vinegar

1 cup peanut or canola oil

¼ cup pickle relish

3 tablespoons chopped parsley

1 tablespoon Dijon mustard

Pinch of cayenne

Kosher salt and freshly ground cracked black pepper

Put the egg yolks in the bowl of a food processor or in a blender and, with the machine running, gradually add the vinegar. With the machine still running, gradually add the oil until the mixture is emulsified. Transfer the mayonnaise to a bowl and stir in the relish, parsley, mustard, and cayenne. Season to taste with salt and pepper. Cover and store in the refrigerator for up to 1 day.

# SPICY CORN TARTAR SAUCE

*Makes about 1½ cups*

This tasty tartar sauce is from Emeril Lagasse. See page 8 about egg safety.

1 large egg

1 tablespoon Creole or whole grain mustard

½ teaspoon plus a pinch of kosher salt

1 tablespoon fresh lemon juice

1 cup vegetable oil

1½ teaspoons unsalted butter

½ cup fresh or thawed frozen corn kernels

Pinch of cayenne

¼ cup peeled, seeded, and chopped tomatoes (see page 11)

2 tablespoons chopped green onions, green parts only

1 tablespoon seeded and minced jalapeño pepper

1 tablespoon chopped parsley

1 teaspoon minced garlic

½ teaspoon Emeril's Creole Seasoning (page 23) or other Creole or Cajun seasoning

To make the mayonnaise, combine the egg, mustard, ½ teaspoon salt, and the lemon juice in a food processor or a blender, and process until smooth, about 15 seconds. With the motor running, pour the oil through the feed tube in a slow, steady stream, thinning with a tablespoon of water as needed if the mixture becomes too thick. Transfer to a medium bowl, cover with plastic wrap, and refrigerate until ready to use. Melt the butter in a small skillet over medium-high heat. Add the corn, the pinch of salt, and the cayenne, and cook, stirring occasionally, until the corn is golden brown, 4 to 5 minutes. Remove from the heat and let cool completely.

Add the corn and remaining ingredients to the mayonnaise and mix well. Adjust the seasoning to taste and refrigerate until chilled, about 1 hour, before serving. The sauce will keep refrigerated for up to 1 day.

# LEMON DILL CREAM

1 cup sour cream

½ cup finely chopped fresh
  dill

1 tablespoon fresh lemon juice

1 teaspoon grated lemon zest

Kosher salt and freshly
  ground black pepper

Combine the sour cream, dill, and lemon juice and zest in a small bowl. Season to taste with salt and pepper. Store in the refrigerator until ready to serve.

# FRESH TOMATO RELISH

*Makes about 2 cups*

Classically, you would peel the tomatoes for tomato concassé, the French term for diced fresh tomatoes. But in my opinion, you only need to peel tomatoes if you're planning to cook them, because tomato skins in a cooked dish have an unpleasant texture. When tomatoes are served raw, as in this recipe, the peels don't bother me.

| | | |
|---|---|---|
| 2 to 3 medium-large ripe, flavorful tomatoes (about 1½ pounds) | ⅓ cup picked parsley leaves<br>¼ cup extra virgin olive oil | Kosher salt and freshly ground black pepper |

Core the tomatoes, then cut them in half crosswise. Gently squeeze out some of the seeds and juice. Cut each tomato half into quarters. Set one of the quarters on a work surface, peel side down, and use a sharp paring knife to horizontally slice away all the seed cavities. (You will be left with a flat, smooth wedge of tomato with peel on one side.) Continue with the remaining quarters. Then, with a sharp chef's knife, finely and evenly julienne the tomatoes, or finely dice them.

Put the tomatoes in a bowl, add the parsley and olive oil, and mix. Season to taste with salt and pepper and mix again. It's best to keep the relish at room temperature, and prepare it no more than an hour before you plan to serve it.

# JACQUES PÉPIN'S RED SAUCE

*Makes about ½ cup*

⅓ cup mayonnaise

2 tablespoons ketchup

1 teaspoon wasabi paste (in a tube) or wasabi powder

2 teaspoons fresh squeezed lime juice

1 tablespoon water

Combine all the sauce ingredients in a bowl. Store in the refrigerator.

# CUCUMBER YOGURT

*Makes about 2 cups*

½ large cucumber, peeled
and seeded

Kosher salt

1½ cups plain yogurt

2 tablespoons chopped fresh
cilantro

2 tablespoons chopped fresh
mint

2 tablespoons minced
scallions, white and green
parts

2 teaspoons stemmed, seeded,
and minced jalapeño pepper

½ teaspoon grated lemon
zest

1 tablespoon fresh lemon
juice

Freshly ground black pepper

Grate the cucumber and place it in a strainer set over a bowl. Generously salt the cucumber and let drain for half an hour, then squeeze the liquid out. In a bowl, combine the cucumber, yogurt, cilantro, mint, scallions, jalapeño, and lemon juice and zest. Season to taste with salt and pepper. Store in the refrigerator until ready to serve.

# SPICY REMOULADE

*Makes about 1½ cups*

¾ cup mayonnaise

¼ cup finely chopped celery

2 tablespoons fresh lemon juice

2 tablespoons chopped parsley

1 tablespoon plus 1 teaspoon prepared horseradish

1 tablespoon minced shallot

1 tablespoon whole-grain mustard

1 tablespoon ketchup

2 teaspoons Worcestershire sauce

1½ teaspoons paprika

1 teaspoon Tabasco or to taste

½ teaspoon minced garlic

Kosher salt

Put the mayonnaise in a bowl and add the remaining ingredients. Stir to combine and season to taste with salt. Store in the refrigerator until ready to serve.

# TOMATO-AVOCADO SALSA

*Makes about 2 cups*

1 large ripe tomato

1 ripe but firm avocado

2 tablespoons plus 2 teaspoons thinly sliced chives

2 tablespoons fresh lemon juice

1 tablespoon plus 1 teaspoon grated lemon zest

Kosher salt and freshly ground black pepper

Core the tomato, cut it in half horizontally, and gently squeeze out the seeds and excess juice. Cut the tomatoes into ¼-inch dice and place in a bowl. Cut the avocado in half, remove the pit, and scoop the meat out of the skin, using a large spoon. Cut the avocado into ¼-inch dice and add to the bowl. Add the chives, lemon juice, and lemon zest to the bowl, season to taste with salt and pepper, and stir gently to combine. This salsa is best if you don't make it more than half an hour before you plan to serve it.

# ROASTED TOMATILLO SALSA

8 ounces tomatillos
(2½ cups), husked, rinsed,
and dried

2 teaspoons olive oil plus
1 tablespoon

1 poblano or Anaheim pepper,
roasted, peeled, seeded, and
diced (see page 62)

2 tablespoons chopped fresh
cilantro leaves

1 tablespoon finely chopped
red onion

1 tablespoon fresh lime juice

1 teaspoon chopped garlic

1 teaspoon pureed canned
chipotle peppers in adobo
or more to taste (see
page 8)

Kosher salt and freshly
ground black pepper

Preheat the oven to 400°F. Combine the tomatillos with the 2 teaspoons olive oil in a pan and place in the oven for about 10 minutes, tossing them around a couple times, until softened and lightly browned here and there. Allow the tomatillos to cool slightly, then put them on a cutting board and chop coarsely. Put the tomatillos in a sieve and drain off and discard all the liquid. Combine the drained tomatillos, the poblano, cilantro, onion, lime juice, garlic, chipotle, and the remaining 1 tablespoon olive oil. Season to taste with salt and pepper.

# AJI AMARILLO SAUCE

*Makes about 1 cup*

½ cup pineapple juice

1 yellow bell pepper, roasted, peeled, and seeded (see page 62)

¼ cup fresh lime juice

2 tablespoons aji Amarillo yellow pepper sauce, such as Amazonas brand (available in Latino markets)

2 tablespoons olive oil

1 teaspoon minced garlic

Kosher salt

Put the pineapple juice in a small saucepan over medium heat and bring to a boil. Simmer the juice, reducing the heat as necessary, until it is thick and syrupy. (You should have a few tablespoons syrup.) Coarsely chop the bell pepper. Put the bell pepper in a blender and add the pineapple syrup, lime juice, aji Amarillo, olive oil, and garlic. Blend until smooth. Season to taste with salt.

# CLAM AIOLI

*Makes about 1½ cups*

1 large egg yolk

1 teaspoon Dijon mustard

3 tablespoons minced garlic

¼ cup extra virgin olive oil

1 cup bottled clam juice

Kosher salt and freshly ground black pepper

Combine the egg yolk with the mustard and garlic in a bowl. Gradually and slowly add the olive oil, whisking constantly, until the mixture emulsifies into a mayonnaise. (Note: You could make this amount of mayonnaise in a mini food processor, but it is too small a quantity to emulsify in a blender or larger food processor.)

Meanwhile, put the clam juice in a small saucepan and bring to a boil. Remove from the heat and allow to cool for a few minutes. Pour the clam juice into a blender, add the aioli, and blend until smooth. The sauce will be thin. Season to taste with salt and pepper. Pour the sauce into a container and keep warm in a saucepan of hot (not simmering) water. Serve immediately.

# SPICY CHIPOTLE MAYONNAISE

*Makes about 1¼ cups*

This easy-to-make spicy mayo comes from Nancy Silverton's *Twist of the Wrist*.

1 cup mayonnaise

2 tablespoons fresh lemon juice or more

2 tablespoons extra virgin olive oil

¼ cup finely chopped fresh cilantro leaves

1½ tablespoons pureed canned chipotle peppers in adobo (see page 8)

2 teaspoons minced garlic or more

1 teaspoon kosher salt or more

Put the mayonnaise in a small bowl. Use a whisk to stir in the lemon juice and olive oil. Add the cilantro, chipotle, garlic, and salt and stir to combine. Add more lemon juice, garlic, or salt to taste. Store in the refrigerator until ready to serve.

# SAKE SAUCE

*Makes about 1 cup*

½ cup sake

¼ cup soy sauce

¼ cup rice vinegar

1 tablespoon sugar

1 small serrano pepper, seeded and finely chopped

¼ teaspoon minced garlic

1 tablespoon finely chopped green onion, white part only

In a small pan, combine the sake, soy sauce, vinegar, sugar, serrano, and garlic. Warm over medium heat until the sugar dissolves. Remove from the heat, and allow to cool. Add the green onion.

# LIME DIPPING SAUCE

*Makes about ½ cup*

This is **Wild Ginger's** version of nuoc cham, the **Vietnamese** dipping sauce.

3 tablespoons Asian fish sauce

2 tablespoons water

1 tablespoon plus 1 teaspoon
fresh squeezed lime juice

1 tablespoon sugar

2 teaspoons sambal
(see page 10)

½ teaspoon minced garlic

½ teaspoon minced fresh dill

½ teaspoon minced fresh
mint

½ teaspoon minced fresh
Thai basil or regular basil

Combine all the sauce ingredients in a small bowl and stir.

# FENNEL MAYONNAISE

*Makes about ¾ cup*

See page 8 about egg safety.

1 large egg yolk

1 tablespoon plus 1 teaspoon
  dry mustard

2 teaspoons cider vinegar

2 teaspoons brown sugar

1 teaspoon fresh
  lemon juice

1 teaspoon fennel seeds,
  ground (see page 10)

⅔ cup peanut or canola oil

Kosher salt

Combine the egg yolk, mustard, vinegar, sugar, lemon juice, and fennel seeds in the bowl of a medium food processor, mini processor, or blender. Slowly add the oil while the machine is running until the mixture thickens and emulsifies. Season to taste with salt. Store in the refrigerator for up to 1 day.

# RED PEPPER ROUILLE

*Makes about 1½ cups*

2 red bell peppers, roasted, peeled, and seeded (see page 62)

2 cloves garlic

2 anchovy fillets, packed in salt or oil

2 slices French bread, crusts removed

2 teaspoons fresh lemon juice

¼ cup extra virgin olive oil

Kosher salt

Freshly ground black pepper

Combine the bell peppers, garlic, anchovies, and bread in the bowl of a food processor and process until well blended. With the machine running, add the lemon juice and olive oil through the feed tube and process until smooth. Season to taste with salt and pepper. Transfer the rouille to a bowl and set aside, or store in the refrigerator for up to 1 week.

# INDEX